Susan Yoxall
12-19

D0323789

To

....

From

....

Date

....

SUSAN GOSS

We're Still in This

90 HEALTHY TRUTHS
FOR HAPPY RELATIONSHIPS

We're Still in This: 90 Healthy Truths for Happy Relationships
© 2019 DaySpring Cards, Inc. All rights reserved.
First Edition, August 2019

Published by:

DaySpring

P.O. Box 1010
Siloam Springs, AR 72761
dayspring.com

Scripture quotations marked NASB are taken from the NEW AMERICAN STANDARD
BIBLE®, © Copyright The Lockman Foundation. (www.lockman.org)

Scripture quotations marked NLT are taken from the Holy Bible, New Living
Translation, copyright © 1996, 2004, 2007 by Tyndale House Foundation. Used by
permission of Tyndale House Publishers, Inc., Carol Stream, Illinois 60188. All rights
reserved.

Scripture quotations marked ESV are taken from the ESV Bible® (The Holy Bible,
English Standard Version®) copyright ©2001 by Crossway Bibles, a publishing
ministry of Good News Publishers. Used by permission. All rights reserved.

Scripture quotations marked TLB are taken from © The Living Bible with permission
from Tyndale House Publishers, Inc., Wheaton, IL.

Scripture quotations marked The Message are taken from The Message. © Eugene
Peterson. Permission from NavPress.

Scripture quotations marked The Voice are taken from The Voice™. Copyright ©
2008 by Ecclesia Bible Society. All rights reserved.

Scripture marked AMP are taken from the Amplified® Bible, © 1954, 1958, 1962, 1964,
1965, 1987 by The Lockman Foundation. Used by permission. (www.Lockman.org)

Written by: Susan Goss
Cover Design: Gearbox
Typeset by: Greg Jackson of thinkpen.design
Printed in China

Prime: 89893
ISBN: 978-1-68408-621-4

TABLE OF CONTENTS

Introduction

WE were created for relationships. God, in His genius and creativity, designed us to both need Him and to need each other. The only problem with relationships... is people...right? We can do and say the strangest things to each other. But God says that we are to love each other as we love ourselves; that our love for Him should be reflected in our love for others. So how do we do that? This devotional book is chocked full of practical, tangible takeaways for you to apply today! Every difficult relationship I have ever had, I have totally had to rely on Jesus because I couldn't fix it, control it, or will it to health on my own. Each entry gives hope, encouragement, and sometimes a little therapeutic message along the way, but one thing for sure you will know after reading this book is that you are not alone. I am passionate about a Savior that is passionate about His people. I pray His heart connects to yours as you read it.

—Susan Goss

Press Rewind

Be humble. Be gentle. Be patient.
Tolerate one another in an atmosphere thick with love.
Make every effort to preserve the unity the Spirit
has already created, with peace binding you together.

EPHESIANS 4:2—3 THE VOICE

SOMETIMES people feel the great need to punch rewind and start the conversation all over again! That just means they're human. Whether it is their spouse, friend, boss, or child, there is not a relationship in the world that has not been in need of a rewind button that slows us down long enough to reflect on a conversation gone bad. We ask ourselves, "Did I just say that?" or "Did I just hear that?" Well, here is the deal—there is a God, and we are not Him. So therefore, with every relationship we are in, we are dealing with imperfect people. We are imperfect, and they are imperfect. Learning to embrace each other's imperfections can only be done by asking God to love through us. It rolls off the tongue easily, but it's not as easy to live out. But there's good news! God is in the business of restoring relationships. God gently reminds us to "tolerate one another in an atmosphere thick with love."

Tangible Takeaway ···

The universal phrase "stop, drop, and roll" can be applied here. "Stop" means stop! Slow down, take a deep breath, and stop to think about what was said or what you heard. You may need to clarify by being curious and asking questions. "Drop" means drop to your knees metaphorically or in real time to pray and ask God what next steps need to take place. You may need to say you are sorry, or you may need to do some forgiveness work. Now it is time to "roll" it over to God and ask Him to intervene in and through you as only He can do.

You Choose

Words kill, words give life;
they're either poison or fruit—you choose.

PROVERBS 18:21 THE MESSAGE

HAVE you ever been told you were sensitive or lazy? Or maybe the words you heard were more like worthless, stubborn, impatient, or even stupid? To the contrary, have you ever been told that you were kind and loving? Or maybe smart, hardworking, responsible...have you ever been told that you were a gift? Words matter! In fact, Proverbs says our words bring life or death, and we get to choose. Have you ever had words hurt you to your core? I have. In fact, words have brought poison to my entire body, making me question everything—even at times who I am. You see, when you're repeatedly told "you're lazy" or "you're shy" or "you're too sensitive"... you soon start to believe it, even if it's not true. On the other hand, if someone says, "you're kind" or "you're dependable," "you're loyal," "you're smart," or "you're such a gift," that self-fulfilling prophecy gives life and bears fruit. Are you choosing your words wisely? Are you filling your loved ones with life-giving words? Or are you using your words to bring pain and hurt? Remember, you choose—poison or fruit?

Tangible Takeaway

In your current relationships, ask yourself: "Are my words bringing death (poison) or life (fruit) to others?" And when others speak over you, ask the question, "Are these words true (from God), or are these words lies (only man's opinion)?" Because a self-fulfilling prophecy can be man's opinion only...so ask God first! You want to both speak in truth and receive the truth that brings freedom!

Throw Away the Ledger

These things I have spoken to you so that My joy may be in you, and that your joy may be made full.

JOHN 15:11 NASB

LISTS, ledgers, and relationships—can they coexist? Does a square peg fit into a round hole? If the goal for a relationship is to be healthy, then lists and ledgers cannot be part of it. No doubt about it, a good grocery list is essential when going to the store—it keeps a person focused, organized, and is a great time (and money) saver. But when applied to people, that same list can turn critical, judgmental, and damaging very quickly. It is human nature to look for things that are wrong... and so it happens. So whether family, friend, or foe, one should examine and determine why there is a list. Is it a matter of not liking them, observing things about them that should change, or wanting them to do something for "us"? In essence, a ledger is being kept on those relationships, wanting them to change so "we" can be happier. That's unhealthy for everyone individually and for the relationship. God is where JOY is found and a true sense of self because it's in HIM, not from others! People fail us all the time, so throw away the ledger. God never fails! IT'S IN HIM ALONE where grace abounds!

Tangible Takeaway ·····································

If you love lists, that's awesome because it's a great way to keep organized, know where you're going, and what to get once you're there! Just become keenly aware if you transition from a "to do" or "grocery" list to a "people" list that looks a lot like a ledger as mentioned above. If you find yourself with a ledger on your hands, turn that ledger on its heel by asking God to help you write down at least five positive thoughts about that person and then surprise them with a note of encouragement by giving them your "list."

This Is Us

*In everything give thanks; for this is God's will
for you in Christ Jesus.*

I THESSALONIANS 5:18 NASB

MANY say that the antidote to bitterness is thankfulness. They are polar opposites, making it almost impossible for the two to coexist. But can we choose thankfulness over bitterness?

The Israelites give us a great example of being both thankful and bitter. When God provided manna (miraculous supplied food) and a way out of slavery, the Israelites were thankful; but when they began to start hating that same food (manna), they started complaining to the point of becoming bitter. They quickly forgot about the slavery and the severe punishment they had endured.

This is us. In our relationships we do the same as the Israelites and forget about the history we have shared with each other. But what if thankfulness is the antidote to bitterness? Scripture says, "In everything give thanks; for this is God's will for you in Christ Jesus." In. Everything.

Give. Thanks. It is impossible to be thankful and bitter at the same time. You can either be thankful or bitter—it is your choice. Sometimes bitterness might seem like the easy way out, but interestingly enough, thankfulness kills bitterness. Thankfulness wins. It beats out bitterness every time. Try it and see. In our relationships it is important for us to choose thankfulness, "for this is God's will for you in Christ Jesus."

Tangible Takeaway

Thanksgiving is a holiday season; thankfulness, however, is a condition of the heart. Get with God and examine your heart. Is your heart full of thankfulness or bitterness? Are you choosing the easy way out? It takes more energy to be thankful because sometimes you don't want to be. But the more you practice thankfulness, the more natural it becomes to you. Begin the practice of thankfulness today and start killing bitterness.

Playing Mind Games

So we're not giving up. How could we! Even though
on the outside it often looks like things are falling apart
on us, on the inside, where God is making new life,
not a day goes by without His unfolding grace.
II CORINTHIANS 4:16 THE MESSAGE

GENERALLY speaking, what is said is never what is heard. Thinking about this statement makes one realize *that's really true* because more times than not, we assume the worst and then we start acting out what we *think* we heard. It's like we instantly become mind readers! Then we are mad at our spouse, friend, or colleague, and they might not even know anything is wrong. Why? Because no one stopped to clarify or even ask the question, "Did you mean that? Because I heard this." All to find out at the end of the very long and exhausting day of feeling angry, hurt, bitter, and resentful that we find out *we were the ones who were wrong*.

When we do finally ask, we might hear back, "That's not what I meant at all; this is my heart, this is what I said, and I'm so glad you asked instead of continuing to assume the worst." It's exhausting to try to read minds, to assume the worst, to brood all day. It's so much easier to stop and clarify the moment something doesn't sound right or just sounds out of character from the one delivering the message. God is a God of order, NOT confusion. So seek order today and, when in question, stop and clarify.

Tangible Takeaway

When in doubt about what was heard...stop and be curious. Ask clarifying questions immediately! Do not wait and let your mind take you places you don't need to go. God only speaks truth, so ask Him to speak through you. He is a God of order.

Don't be shy. Pray for God's confidence...the relationship is worth finding out the truth.

Human Beings Not Human Doings

Come to Me, all who are weary and heavy-laden, and I will give you rest. Take My yoke upon you and learn from Me, for I am gentle and humble in heart, and you will find rest for your souls. For My yoke is easy and My burden is light.

MATTHEW 11:28–30 NASB

DO you ever think to yourself, *I wish people knew me for who I am instead of for what I do?* There is an often-used quote that says, "We are human *beings*, NOT human *doings*." Oh, that we would believe that powerful, rich statement! If we were completely honest with ourselves, we might even use the term human *strivers* to describe what's really going on in a world where we often hear, "That's great; now let's see if you can do it better next time." And if we were really honest with ourselves, we might acknowledge that we are striving even in our relationships, which leaves us wondering, "Will I ever be able to work hard enough to get it right? Or is it me? Am

I good enough?" Humans are getting tired, worn out, and overwhelmed trying, the vast majority of the time, to meet unrealistic expectations—not only at a professional level but also in their personal relationships. And for what? For the most part, the approval of man. God has a rebuttal to the world's way of thinking, and it turns human striving on its ear. God always sees the true us *first*. He sees who we are as human *beings*. If we are only interested in what others think, we'll be on a hamster wheel for the rest of our lives. If we first, however, realize our identity rests in Christ, then we'll know we are not primarily human *strivers* and human *doings*, but human *beings*. Created in the image of God. Knowing this truth frees us from the burden of doing to find rest in our relationships.

Tangible Takeaway

Take the Scripture from today and read it out loud. Make it personal by inserting your name to make it real in your life. "Come to Me, (place your name), and I will give you rest." It's such a comfort knowing God's Word is personal.

Give Extra Grace

So I give you a new command: Love each other
deeply and fully. Remember the ways that I have
loved you, and demonstrate your love for others
in those same ways. Everyone will know you as My
followers if you demonstrate your love to others.

JOHN 13:34—35 THE VOICE

"PEOPLE are funny, and I don't mean *ha ha*." Upon hearing this quote, one of my dear friends said, "Susan, you've got to go on the road with that statement."

So why do people relate so passionately to this quote? Because we're people too...and people can say and do the strangest things. We all have challenging people in our lives who need extra grace.

Years ago before I was a therapist, I was an elementary school administrator and the school secretary used to say, "Susan, some people are just turned differently."

All these statements are true and bring us back to my original quote, "People are funny, and I don't mean *ha ha*." Which is a quirky little way of saying, nobody's perfect. Although sometimes in relationships, we sure do expect them to be, don't we? But we're not perfect either...not one of us! We all stand in desperate need of God's abundant grace. So next time someone annoys you, try listening to that silent voice inside your head saying, "Give Extra Grace."

Tangible Takeaway

Anytime you encounter someone that requires extra grace and you desire to represent Jesus well to them, remember these things:

This isn't about you...but about God in you.
God loves them as much as He loves you.
Ask God to love them through you.
Ask God to grow you through this encounter.
Praise God for His full and deep love for His people.

Boomerang Kind of Love

We Christians have no veil over our faces; we can be mirrors that brightly reflect the glory of the Lord. And as the Spirit of the Lord works within us, we become more and more like Him.

II CORINTHIANS 3:18 TLB

A friend asked me recently what I thought reflected health in any given relationship. That question led to a great discussion, and this is where it landed: I deeply desire for my relationship with God to be reflected in my relationships with His people. That represents health to me! The biggest problem with this is the fact that we as humans are fickle and fallible. Have you noticed that when things are going well, it's much easier to let the supernatural work of Jesus come through? But when someone causes you pain, yells at you, or provokes you, it's easier to let the "natural" human self come through.

For example, when someone provokes or triggers

me, my response to them says more about me and my relationship to God than it says about them! I know, the first time I heard that, I really had to think about it. My response to another human being is not based on their behavior but on where I am in my relationship with Jesus. Therefore, my anchor, my security, has to be Christ—it simply cannot be in a human being that is fickle and fallible. God is neither. God is never changing and rock solid! I must stay connected to God in order to reflect Him to others. I guess you could call it a "boomerang kind of love" with God! Because if I am secure in my relationship with Him, it comes back to me in the form of healthy relationships.

Tangible Takeaway

Do your relationships with others reflect your relationship with God? Is your relationship with God growing and healthy? Take inventory of the relationships in your life (have pen and paper ready to process), and ask God to show you next steps.

You Can't Judge a Book by Its Cover

For the LORD sees not as a man sees:
man looks on the outward appearance,
but the LORD looks on the heart.

I SAMUEL 16:7 ESV

DID you have a best friend growing up? Think back to one of yours. I did, and her name was Ruthie. We were inseparable. "Two peas in a pod" as my grandmother would say. Ruthie was special in so many ways. She was adventurous, happy, kind, a great friend...and she was also totally deaf. Ruthie communicated by reading lips, and I seemed to understand her better than almost anyone. We were more alike than different. Often I was her interpreter for those who couldn't understand her form of communication. She always said she "felt heard by me." And in return, I felt understood by Ruthie from the inside out because I was a young, chubby, elementary girl who looked a lot different than the other girls in our class. We saw each other with the same eyes that Jesus sees us. He doesn't look at our outward appearances, but in our hearts.

What culture tells us about appearance is different from what God tells us. The world tells us beauty is perfection, but Scripture tells us, "For the LORD sees not as man sees: man looks on the outward appearance, but the LORD looks on the heart."

Tangible Takeaway

How do you define beauty?

Who influences you...God or the world (social media)?

Are you just looking at the outward appearance of others (comparison), or are you looking at their hearts?

Ask God to help you see others through His eyes.

What about Me?

Therefore encourage one another
and build up one another,
just as you also are doing.

I THESSALONIANS 5:11 NASB

PAUL makes it very clear in I Thessalonians 5:11 that we are to encourage and build one another up. One would think that is the easiest thing in the world to do, especially when it comes to encouraging those we love, but sadly for many...encouraging words just don't tend to *roll off the tongue* like you would think. We live in a social-media-saturated world whose byline mainly screams out, "What about ME?" And while social media platforms can be used to connect believers, send out prayer requests, and share news with your friends and family, it can also set the stage for self-centeredness. This condition of self-centeredness makes it more difficult to be happy for someone else's success while we are struggling to find our own. Online media is sometimes focused on serving us while encouragement is focused on serving others. But that is exactly what

Paul is referencing in our Scripture today. "Therefore encourage one another and build up one another, just as you also are doing." And here's the funny thing about encouragement: the more you encourage someone else, the more *you* feel encouraged. It's beautiful how that works, isn't it? And it's also God's way.

Tangible Takeaway

We need to spend more time focusing on encouraging and building up one another than emphasizing self—changing our "what about me" to "what about others." Honestly ask yourself: "Do I spend more time promoting myself than encouraging others?" Personalize today's Scripture by adding your name, and be encouraged through encouraging.

"Therefore, (your name) , encourage one another and, (your name) , build up one another, just as you also are doing" (I Thessalonians 5:11 NASB).

Family laughs are the BEST laughs...starting with self. I think you have to be able to laugh at yourself first! I can say and do the dumbest things, and if any of my family "happens" to catch it, boy do I hear about it and we all get a big belly laugh out of it! But what goes around comes around if you can laugh at yourself. Make it fun!

—SUSAN GOSS

Understanding Our True Enemy

There are "friends" who destroy each other, but a real friend sticks closer than a brother.

PROVERBS 18:24 NLT

IN her book *Uninvited*, Lysa TerKeurst states, "We have an enemy—and it's NOT each other!"[1] This is such a great statement, and it is also true. But think about it for a second...have you ever treated someone like they were your enemy? A spouse, a friend, a child? It sounds counterintuitive to loving them, doesn't it? If you love them, why would you treat them that way? In today's Scripture we read that, "There are 'friends' who destroy each other...." So it makes sense that in our relationships, because of our humanness, we end up treating each other like the enemy by assuming the worst of each other. At times we even take on the role of *mind reader*—somehow giving permission to assume (or make up) what we want to believe about something or someone without ever asking or clarifying. This deadly pattern of assuming the worst without asking questions is a tactic of the true enemy, Satan, who hates healthy relationships. First Peter 5:8 (The Voice) states that "the devil is prowling around outside like a roaring lion, just waiting and hoping for the chance to devour someone." It bears repeating: "We have an enemy—and it's NOT each other!"

Tangible Takeaway

If the enemy is trying to break your relationships:

- *Don't assume the worst.*
- *Literally stop and say to the other, "I am not your enemy."*
- *Remind each other who the real enemy is.*
- *Remind each other Whose you are and that God is ALWAYS FOR your relationship.*

Sacrifice "Winning"

Live in true devotion to one another, loving
each other as sisters and brothers. Be first to
honor others by putting them first.

ROMANS 12:10 THE VOICE

RELATIONSHIPS vs. Being Right—now there is an intriguing statement! Can the two coexist? It seems the answer is yes and no. If a person values *relationship* more than they value *being right*—well, then, the answer is a quick yes. If not, it's a fast no. But doesn't choosing relationship over having to be right all the time seem obvious? No. Humans seem to have this intrinsic need to control something. We know we're right, and so we go on a mission to prove it! The tension is, you might be the one who is, in fact, right—but you also might lose the relationship over fighting the battle to prove it! When talking about healthy relationships, the word *sacrifice* will come into play. Sacrifice usually has something to do with *us* doing something *for someone else* that mostly is outside of our comfort level, but we do it anyway because it benefits those we love and the relationship we're in. That sometimes means we sacrifice "winning" the right to be right in order to save the relationship. Do you choose relationship over being right?

Tangible Takeaway

For this Tangible Takeaway, a scenario will be given as an example to follow:

It may be true that every time the in-laws come over, they trigger you by pinching your cheeks hard and kissing you on the forehead multiple times; and it may be true that you hate that—but in order to maintain relationship with your spouse and your in-laws and the culture in which they were raised and learned those things, you sacrifice your irritation and uncomfortableness in order to maintain harmony within the family system. So how does this scenario show choosing relationship over being right? The person in this scenario could have said, "Stop! I don't want you to touch me. That bothers me when you kiss me. It's weird. It hurts me when you pinch so hard. It invades my privacy—it's my body, not yours." Instead they embraced the greeting, knowing it would be short-lived and how important it was to their family by putting relationship first.

Remember the Golden Rule

In everything, therefore, treat people the same way you want them to treat you, for this is the Law and the Prophets.

MATTHEW 7:12 NASB

MATTHEW 7:12, known as *The Golden Rule*, rolls off the tongue like water off a duck's back and has long been known as "the standard" for how to treat others the way God intended for lasting, healthy relationships. So why is it so hard to do? When someone is kind to you, it's easy to be kind back. But let's be real—when someone is unkind to you, is your first inclination to be kind back to them? *Hence the tension of The Golden Rule.* But God says do it anyway! God designed us to need Him so that we might seek Him, and that means daily and in all relationships. I don't know about you, but I need Him desperately when someone wrongs me and I am left to respond *the way I want to be treated.* It's not natural for me to *not* want to defend or say something I might regret later. I need God to love them through me when I might not *feel* like loving them but know that I should. God knows our struggle. Let Him work...let Him love others through you! Don't allow The Golden Rule to just become a verse to memorize, but let it be transformative in your life as God is allowed to live it out in you.

Tangible Takeaway

You would think this would be the easiest Tangible Takeaway yet, but if The Golden Rule were easy to follow, we would all already be treating each other as we want to be treated. It's just not that easy because we're humans, and humans are very hard on humans! So here are some helpful tips:

1. *Ask God to help you see ALL humans through His lens (He loves them ALL).*
2. *Put your feet in their shoes (and meet them where THEY are, not where you might want or wish them to be).*
3. *Give grace! Absolutely none of us deserve it, but ALL of us are freely given it because of Jesus, so pass it on!*
4. *Be you. Pray. Jesus is your model. If some reject you, well, you're in good company. They rejected Him too— all the way to the cross where He demonstrated His unfathomable love for mankind.*

Is Humility Countercultural?

Lay yourself bare, facedown to the ground, in humility before the Lord; and He will lift your head so you can stand tall.

JAMES 4:10 THE VOICE

HUMILITY. Now that's a word you just don't see or hear much about on any kind of social media or TV programming. There are not many movie scripts full of lines like "love your enemies" (Matthew 5:44) or "love your neighbor as yourself" (Matthew 22:39) and certainly not "turn the other cheek" (Matthew 5:39). Sadly, it sometimes seems as if humility is becoming countercultural. And in many cases, children are being raised to learn, know, and develop their strengths and push aside their weaknesses. This behavior has grave spiritual repercussions because God literally designed us to lean on Him.

When we try to have healthy relationships using our own strength, we will fail every time. When we try to lead without Him, we will fail every time! Satan knows where we are vulnerable, weak, and defenseless and attacks us in those weakest, most vulnerable areas—it's his job! Scripture is clear, "Stay alert! Watch out for your great enemy, the devil. He prowls around like a roaring lion, looking for someone to devour" (I Peter 5:8 NLT). But fear not, mighty warrior of God, "He who is in you is greater than he who is in the world" (I John 4:4 ESV). God is always for you! Being humble literally takes *us* out of the equation so God can work! True humility says, "I can't, but HE CAN."

Tangible Takeaway

The end of Psalm 139 reads, "And see if there be any hurtful way in me, and lead me in the everlasting way" (Psalm 139:24 NASB). In the margins of my Bible, I translate this verse as, "show me me as You see me."

With a sincere heart before God, ask Him to reveal your heart as He sees it. Be ready because He will!

I call these Mirror Moments with God, and they are life-giving if you allow them to be.

Hold Your Horses

Slow down. Take a deep breath. What's the hurry?
Why wear yourself out? Just what are you after anyway?
JEREMIAH 2:25 THE MESSAGE

HAVE you ever been mad at a coworker or even your boss to then go home and take that anger out on someone else? As the more classic example puts it, "You're mad at the boss so you go home and kick the dog!" It's called Displacement. Or, as Gerald Corey puts it in his book *Theory and Practice of Counseling and Psychotherapy (7th Edition)*: "*one way to cope with anxiety is to discharge impulses by shifting from a threatening object to a 'safer target.'*"[2] Displacement consists of directing energy toward another object or person when the original object or person is inaccessible. For example, the meek man who feels intimidated by his boss comes home and unloads inappropriate hostility onto his children. Being able to identify displaced anger or displacement is a very important piece in order to begin a healthy start for *repair*. Knowing whether the anger is brought into the present relationship from unfinished business somewhere else or if it's from the current relationship is critical to the recovery of that relationship. Jeremiah 2:25 states, "Slow down. Take a deep breath. What's the hurry? Why wear yourself out? Just what are you after anyway?" A perfect reminder for us to slow down and ask ourselves *and* each other...what's *really* going on here?

Tangible Takeaway

Next time you are "triggered" by someone or a specific circumstance, ask yourself this question: God, what's really going on in my heart? Reveal to me my heart as You see me. Then pray out loud Jeremiah 2:25: "Slow down. Take a deep breath. What's the hurry? Why wear yourself out? Just what are you after anyway?" Now personalize this Scripture and turn it into a prayer: "(your name), slow down. Take a deep breath. What's the hurry? Why wear yourself out? Just what are you after anyway?"

Connection

Rejoice with those who rejoice,
and weep with those who weep.

ROMANS 12:15 NASB

MEET people where they are. Don't try to change them, fix them, or correct them, but instead recognize where they are in that very moment. Meet them in their greatest joy or deepest pain and at times when words simply will not form in your mouth. Then just acknowledge, "I don't know what to say to you right now, but what I do know is that I want to be here for you." When you are able to say that to another human being, they immediately feel connected to you, understood by you, and they don't feel alone anymore...and that feels like a warm blanket on a cold, rainy night. God has His own version of "meeting people where they are," and it's found in Romans 12:15: "Rejoice with those who rejoice, and weep with those who weep." How beautiful...how perfect...how just like God! This extraordinary passage of Scripture implies that if there is reason to celebrate, then celebrate and celebrate wildly. And if there is reason for weeping, then

deal with! Sometimes I have to take off work for several days because they are so bad...I hate them!" The reason this script is an example of "how not to show empathy" is because the person that responded made it about themselves, not about the person who had the headache and reached out. Empathy connects—this script *doesn't* connect.

How TO show empathy:

Someone says: "I don't know if I can work today because I just found out early this morning that my mom has cancer and it's already stage four. I'm devastated and don't think I'll be worth anything today." Then you respond, "Wow, I'm so sorry to hear that. I don't know what to say except that I am so thankful you felt comfortable enough to tell me, and I want you to know that I am here for you. Do whatever you need to do today." Empathy connects—this script connects!

Empathy builds connection because it feels what others feel.

Tangible Takeaway ··

Although awkward at first, empathy can be learned:
Using the "how to" scenario above, practice using empathy in front of the mirror, or if given the opportunity, role play with another. Now change the scenario of not showing empathy into a "how to" scenario. Make it fun!

Created for Connection

Then the LORD God said,
"It is not good for the man to be alone.
I will make a helper who is just right for him."

GENESIS 2:18 NLT

A basic human need is to be heard and understood—but in a world where glances have taken the place of eye-to-eye contact and text messaging has replaced human conversation, is that still possible? With the help of empathy, the answer is yes. By its definition, empathy is the ability to understand and share the feelings of another.

The Lord God said in Genesis 2:18, "It is not good for the man to be alone. I will make a helper who is just right for him." And then God said that it was *good* (Genesis 1:31), thus "relationships" became a part of humanity's basic design. Please don't miss that beautiful fact. We were never meant to do life alone—quite the opposite in fact.

The use of empathy is critical when it comes to building connection. My grandmother would say at times, "We don't know what it's like to walk in someone else's shoes, but try to imagine literally putting your feet in their shoes and living their lives for a while, and then you'll see them differently." Sounds like my grandmother was trying to teach a heaping dose of empathy, and those words of wisdom still ring true today. Understanding who you are *with* is important for connection, so be curious, listen carefully, and be sensitive to the feelings of who you might come in contact with.

Tangible Takeaway

As you develop a language for empathy, pray Psalm 19:14 (NASB), "Let the words of my mouth and the meditation of my heart be acceptable in Your sight."

To help a heart of empathy, grab a piece of paper and write down as many Scriptures as you can find that help your connection with others. You can start with Psalm 19:14.

I Love You, If

For God so loved the world, that He gave His only begotten Son, that whoever believes in Him shall not perish, but have eternal life.

JOHN 3:16 NASB

WE all receive different messages from our "family of origin" growing up. We are all products of how we were raised...both good and bad. Many received messages associated with love that were conditional—messages like, *I love you if you do what I ask of you*; if you don't, then the message associated with love is, *I withhold love*. One soon learns in that environment: *if I please and achieve, I am loved; if I don't, I am not.* The message of that kind of love is conditional. The message of unconditional love says simply, *I love you, period!* No conditions—*I love you for who you are and will provide a safe environment around you to thrive and grow at your pace with established boundaries at each natural stage of maturity.* Unconditional love gives without expecting anything back.

Christ was, is, and will always be the quintessential example of what unconditional love looks like. He never one time said to anyone, "Hey, you, go get cleaned up. Fix that problem of yours first and then come follow Me." To the tax collector that everyone despised, He said, "Let's have dinner" (Luke 5:27–32). To the Samaritan woman going to a well to draw water at an inconspicuous time of day so that no one would see her—He not only spoke to her but also told her things about herself that only she would have known, opening the door for Jesus to share about the True Living Water which will allow her to never thirst again (John 4:7–26). Jesus exudes love because He is love! Jesus is our go-to model when we are struggling to show another person unconditional love—because while we were sinners, He died for us (Romans 5:8)!

Tangible Takeaway

Rewrite this very familiar passage of Scripture (John 3:16), personalizing it, then read out loud as follows:

"For God so loved (your name) , that He gave (your name) His only begotten Son, that (your name) shall not perish, but have eternal life."

*What we say is content…
how we say it is the
process. If content is
important, then process
is essential.*

—SUSAN GOSS

Comparison Breeds Discontent

Make a careful exploration of who you are and the work
you have been given, and then sink yourself into that.
Don't be impressed with yourself. Don't compare yourself
with others. Each of you must take responsibility for
doing the creative best you can with your own life.

GALATIANS 6:4—5 THE MESSAGE

COMPARISON breeds discontent. From the frivolous to the serious, it's true. If someone buys a new pair of shoes but walks in the room and sees the shoes someone else has on and likes them better, they're suddenly discontent (frivolous... but sometimes true). They just compared their shoes to someone else's shoes. More seriously, one shows up for family pictures at church realistically mismatched and missing three buttons and another family is color coordinated wearing the latest trends and looking "picture perfect." They immediately feel "not good enough" because comparison breeds discontent.

Scripture says, "For where jealousy and selfish ambition exist, there is disorder and every evil thing" (James 3:16 NASB). Why not make a conscious decision to turn away from jealousy and selfish ambition and turn to fueling joy and seeking to find what makes you content? Let's find our lane and flourish in it. Not our neighbor's lane, but our lane.

Tangible Takeaway

Comparison can be good or bad. Comparison when used by God can turn your focus away from self and what you want or don't have toward celebrating what you do have with a heart of contentment. You have to have perspective. Use the example below and make your own chart, filling in the blanks with "good" comparison practices and "bad" comparison practices.

Good:

- *Setting goals and then comparing (assessing) how far you have come from last year to current: spiritually, physically, emotionally/mentally.*

Bad:

- *Comparing someone's house and neighborhood to your house and neighborhood and find yourself "wanting…"*

Open Mouth Disease

*The tongue can bring death or life; those who
love to talk will reap the consequences.*

PROVERBS 18:21 NLT

WE'VE probably all had times where we thought, *DID
I JUST SAY THAT?* It's been called *open mouth disease.*
That nails it, don't you think? If we are human, then we
have *open mouth disease* and have opened our mouths
and said to another human something that we wished
we had not said and would desperately love to take
back. It's called human nature, flesh, the fall of man, not
being perfect...you choose! We say things we don't want
to say. And we do not discriminate—we do this to those
we love and to total strangers as well. So how do we
recover? By saying two very short words: "I'm sorry." It's
like a switch being flipped on paving the way to "begin
again." Of course this takes humility on the side of the
offender, which is the process of "letting go" of self and
allowing God to remove all pride involved so that we
can sincerely say, "You know those words I said to you
the other day...this morning...just seconds ago? I'm so

sorry...they came out wrong. It's like at times I have *open mouth disease*....can we start all over?" These words are like salve on a wound to the hearer. Scripture says it best, "Love is patient and kind. Love is not jealous or boastful or proud or rude. It does not demand its own way. It is not irritable, and it keeps no record of being wronged. It does not rejoice about injustice but rejoices whenever the truth wins out. Love never gives up, never loses faith, is always hopeful, and endures through every circumstance" (I Corinthians 13:4–7 NLT).

Tangible Takeaway

Starting the cure for open mouth disease:

Take a piece of paper and a pen or pencil. Write "I'm sorry" at the top of the page. Now spend some time with God and ask Him whose name(s) need to be listed underneath and what next steps He would have you take.

Addicted to Anxiety

Casting all your anxieties on him,
because he cares for you.

I PETER 5:7 ESV

OUR world has quickly become addicted to anxiety. Everyone *has* anxiety, it's just to what degree your body experiences it. When talking about relationships, anxiety definitely becomes a part of that conversation. Difficult relationships bring with them a degree of anxiety, depending on how much we try to control the other person or the situation that caused the difficult relationships in the first place—or both! In essence, when we try to "fix" or "control" another human being, we somehow start assuming the role of God in their lives, and we quickly find out we were never designed for such a role. Thus the anxiety-provoking tension caused by trying to control another's persona. It does not work because there is a God, and we are not Him. As the Scripture says we are to *cast our anxieties on Him because He cares for us*. God is so good! In fact, He *wants* our anxieties cast on Him. So let Him remove the albatross around your neck.

Tangible Takeaway

It is normal to experience anxiety from time to time. The key is learning to deal with it effectively so that it does not paralyze you or interrupt your ability to function normally in your everyday life.

As with any other problem we face, recognizing we have a problem is the first step toward overcoming it. Take time now to talk honestly with God about what makes you anxious and ask Him to help you in your journey toward greater freedom from anxiety. To guide you in your time with God, here is a sample prayer:

"Dear Father, _____ causes me great anxiety. I surrender _____ over to You because You have told me I can. You say in I Peter 5:7 to cast all my anxiety on You, Lord, because You care for me. So, Lord, I am claiming and believing that to be true. Lord, help me."

The Power of Touch

Everyone wanted to touch Jesus
because when they did, power emanated
from Him and they were healed.

LUKE 6:19 THE VOICE

OH, the power of an emanated touch! Jesus represented stability, healing, and belonging with the touch of His hand. The gift of touch differs for each individual. Some prefer a light touch on the hand or shoulder while others a hug or warm embrace. Knowing the art of touch can benefit all relationships. Touch connects humans in a way nothing else really can. Even the world sees touch as a vital part of connection.

Interestingly, *Psychology Today* states that *"When NBA players touch teammates more, they win more."*[3] It makes sense, as it helps them form a strong bond with one another and a sense that they're all connected.

Sometimes words just aren't enough. Touch can elicit a response that words can't.

David Klow, a marriage and family therapist, states, "Non-verbal communication can be a very powerful way to say to your partner, 'I get you.' Cuddling is a way of saying, 'I know how you feel.' It allows us to feel known by our partner in ways that words can't convey."[4]

As humans, we're designed to be touched. When we form a bond with someone, touch is an integral part of that because when we touch, we don't just connect on a physical level, we connect on an emotional and psychological level too.

Charles Dickens said, "Have a heart that never hardens, and a temper that never tires, and a touch that never hurts."

Tangible Takeaway

Practice the gift of touching:

- *If you are a parent, practice stroking your child's hair when they are in your lap.*
- *If you are a spouse, practice touching by holding hands or rubbing your spouse's shoulders, neck, or back.*
- *If you are single, practice stroking your pet while reading a book or watching TV. If you have no pet, practice hugging your friend.*
- *The point is to get out of your comfort zone and to be more intentional and emanate the gift of touch.*

Take a Good Look at Yourself

Why do you look at the speck that is in your brother's eye, but do not notice the log that is in your own eye? Or how can you say to your brother, "Let me take the speck out of your eye," and behold, the log is in your own eye? You hypocrite, first take the log out of your own eye, and then you will see clearly to take the speck out of your brother's eye.

MATTHEW 7:3—5 NASB

EVIL Queen: "Mirror mirror on the wall, who is the fairest one of all?"

Magic Mirror: "Famed is thy beauty, Majesty. But behold, a lovely maid I see. Rags cannot hide her gentle grace. Alas, she is more fair than thee."

This is an iconic line quoted by the Evil Queen in the famous movie *Snow White and the Seven Dwarfs*. The Merriam-Webster dictionary defines a mirror as "something that gives a true representation." Generally speaking, when one looks at their reflection in the mirror physically, light reflects and bounces off the body to provide a true reflection image. Metaphorically speaking, light and truth are basically synonyms because light reflects the truth. So as it relates to us spiritually, as we look in the mirror we pray for a true reflection of light and wisdom. Not wisdom from the world, but godly wisdom. Godly wisdom sees with His eyes, allowing the true reflection of His image to bounce off you toward others. When this happens, we are not as consumed with the speck in our brother's eyes as modeled by the Evil Queen in *Snow White* than we are consumed with our desire to reflect Jesus. May our prayer become *Jesus, Jesus in my heart...let Your light reflect in all I do.*

"Let your light shine before men in such a way that they may see your good works, and glorify your Father who is in heaven" (Matthew 5:16 NASB).

Tangible Takeaway

Use one of the Scriptures from today's devotion, or choose both, and write it out on index cards, sticky notes, or on your mirror with a marker as a reminder to reflect His light!

Choose Happiness

A joyful heart is good medicine, but a
crushed spirit dries up the bones.

PROVERBS 17:22 ESV

THIS Scripture reminds me of my granddaughter, Adeline, who is a very strong-willed (although still adorable) toddler. When Adeline is acting out, frustrated, and angry, my son will stand up and in a strong, firm voice say, "ADELINE, CHOOSE HAPPINESS." (Knowing happiness is the opposite of what currently is going on in Adeline's heart.) It startles her every time and more times than not becomes the perfect distraction to both calm her down and move her on to the next thing.

Oh, how I wish life were that easy! But I do love a good reframe, and it does reflect the much-loved verse, "This is the day which the LORD has made; Let us rejoice and be glad in it" (Psalm 118:24 NASB). Because just like Adeline, when we "act out," we have a choice to make in that very moment—we can be controlled by a *me-* or God-controlled heart. One has a *toddler temper tantrum* inside and what usually comes out of that is anger. The other chooses *self-control* and is able to rejoice and be glad in the moment. Is it possible to really choose happiness? Yes, but it requires daily surrender and self-awareness because there is no lack of opportunity to choose.

Tangible Takeaway

Webster dictionary defines happy as: "Enjoying contentment and well-being; glad, joyous, satisfied, or pleased." The synonym Scripture gives for happiness is joy. Just like Scripture talks about the tongue having the power to bring life or death through the words we choose...likewise we have the power through the Holy Spirit in us to choose our response to others and our circumstances.

In light of today's devotion, how does Proverbs 18:21 apply to choosing happiness? "Words kill, words give life; they're either poison or fruit—you choose" (The Message).

Belly Laugh

God has graced me with the gift of laughter! To be sure,
everyone who hears my story will laugh with me.

GENESIS 21:6 THE VOICE

A good belly laugh may be just what the doctor ordered. And as the research continues to reveal, laughter is a great form of stress relief, and that's no joke. Anybody need a little less stress in your life? So why not share the "gift of laughter" with someone today and see who might be the first to join in on your hilarious, I'm dying, bent-over-crying, laughing-so-hard story! Scripture tells us, "A cheerful heart is good medicine" (Proverbs 17:22 NLT). And let's face it...laughter connects us to each other. It's good for healthy relationships!

"Laughter is a powerful antidote to stress, pain, and conflict. Nothing works faster or more dependably to bring your mind and body back into balance than a good laugh. Humor lightens your burdens, inspires hopes, connects you to others, and keeps you grounded, focused, and alert. It also helps you to release anger and be more forgiving. With so much power to heal and renew, the ability to laugh easily and frequently is a tremendous resource for surmounting problems, enhancing your relationships, and supporting both physical and emotional health. Best of all, this priceless medicine is fun, free, and easy to use." – HelpGuide.org[5]

Wait just a minute...did I just hear a belly laugh?

Tangible Takeaway

This may be THE BEST TANGIBLE TAKEAWAY YET!

1. *Lighten up! Don't take yourself so seriously.*
2. *Make it a goal EVERY DAY to laugh at yourself (because we ALL do the weirdest stuff EVERY DAY).*
3. *Lighten up on others as well...because they do weird stuff too!*
4. *Make it a point to hang around people that have a great sense of humor and make you laugh.*
5. *Have you laughed today? Learn to laugh at yourself and others*, using discernment and grace (*don't laugh at the expense of others), because laughter is a true relationship "gift."*
6. *On your mark...get set...LAUGH!*

Actions Speak Louder Than Words

Put the word into action.
If you think hearing is what matters most,
you are going to find you have been deceived.

JAMES 1:22 THE VOICE

PRESIDENT Abraham Lincoln in the year 1856 confirmed a most familiar proverb to the United States, "Actions speak louder than words." Interestingly, we also find this phrase in Scripture through the words of John in I John 3:18 (NLT), "Dear children, let's not merely say that we love each other; let us show the truth by our actions." Jesus modeled love through action when He took upon Himself the role of servant in John 13. We see Jesus washing the feet of each of His twelve disciples, blessing and demonstrating His endless love as He served alongside them. This was a profound action showing great humility. Even the disciples were taken aback by His devotion to them.

We live in a world where we blurt out *I love you's* without thinking it is time that we take action to back up the meaning behind *I love you*. Too many times love is used as a noun only and not a verb. Love is both. What does *I love you* mean to you? What would the person or persons you are in relationship with say about your *I love you's?* Are they mere words routinely said, or is there action behind their meaning? "For even the Son of Man came not to be served but to serve others and to give His life as a ransom for many" (Matthew 20:28 NLT).

Tangible Takeaway

Do you say I love you?

How many times?

What actions do you take to back that up?

Spend time with God and pray aloud James 1:22, I John 3:18, and Matthew 20:28, personalizing each as you put the word into action, show the truth by your actions, and serve others.

Speaking Others' Language

A new commandment I give to you,
that you love one another:
just as I have loved you,
you also are to love one another.

JOHN 13:34 ESV

JESUS meets people where they are time and time again through the use of parables (short stories used to illustrate a spiritual lesson). His message is received because it was delivered in the language of the hearer. By meeting people where they were, He related the message to the hearers' world. For example, if He happened to be with fishermen, He would talk about casting a net. Yet at another time with carpenters, He would talk about building a foundation. Jesus made the message relatable to whomever He was with. Jesus spoke the language of those He was around because He knew the power of language and its tremendous ability to connect. We, too, have the ability to speak the language of those we want to have a true connection with by being curious and willing to learn their language in order to identify with them. This creates an instant connection. John 13:34 (ESV) tells us, "A new commandment I give to you, that you love one another: just as I have loved you, you also are to love one another." When someone cares enough about you to speak your language, it is a true expression of love...*one to another*.

Tangible Takeaway

One way Jesus loved others was by speaking their language. Think about the people you come in contact with daily. Do you speak their language? Ask God to make you more aware and sensitive to the language of others.

A Cheerful Giver

Giving grows out of the heart—otherwise, you've reluctantly grumbled "yes" because you felt you had to or because you couldn't say "no," but this isn't the way God wants it. For we know that "God loves a cheerful giver."

II CORINTHIANS 9:7 THE VOICE

GOLD, frankincense, and myrrh were the finest the Wise Men had to offer. The Voice Bible commentary indicates that, "These are exceptionally good gifts, for gold is what is given a king, and Jesus is the King of kings; incense is what you'd expect to be given to a priest, and Jesus is the High Priest of all high priests; myrrh ointment is used to heal, and Jesus is a healer. But myrrh is also used to embalm corpses—and Jesus was born to die."[6] If giving grows out of the heart, the Wise Men gave from a heart of worship and praise. Their motive for giving was pure, honest, sincere, and demonstrated their love for Jesus above all else. The Wise Men gave of their best. The motive behind *our* giving should not be self-serving or because we thought we "had to" but to genuinely be concerned about another and what we can do for them.

It is a matter of the heart. Scripture reiterates this in I Samuel 16:7 (NASB), "God sees not as man sees, for man looks at the outward appearance, but the LORD looks at the heart." When giving grows out of the heart, we become *a cheerful giver*, and the recipient of that gift feels cared for and cherished. Ultimately, it is a practical demonstration of love.

Tangible Takeaway

Pray out loud Psalm 139:23 (NLT), "Search me, O God, and know my heart." Ask Him to reveal your heart motive for giving. Now, evaluate where you are in giving:

- *Reluctant giving*
- *Obligated giving*
- *Couldn't say "no" giving*
- *Cheerful giving*

Be refreshed and renewed in the reminder that "God loves a cheerful giver."

friend said that her mom had not said anything about receiving the letter so she asked, "Mom, did you get my letter?" "Oh yes, I just can't talk about it yet...it's too special. I'll start to cry, but I will." My friend's gift did not cost her anything except the cost of a stamp, yet its value is priceless.

If receiving a thoughtful gift makes your heart sing or if you spend hours picking out just the right gift for a friend or loved one, you should know this has nothing to do with materialism, but everything to do with how you show and feel love.

Tangible Takeaway

Think of someone in your life who loves giving and receiving gifts. Pray for God's creativity to come up with just the right gift to make them feel treasured and loved. And remember, it doesn't have to cost a cent.

Undivided Attention

Two are better than one because they have a good return for their labor. For if either of them falls, the one will lift up his companion. But woe to the one who falls when there is not another to lift him up. Furthermore, if two lie down together they keep warm, but how can one be warm alone?

ECCLESIASTES 4:9—11 NASB

THE Merriam-Webster Dictionary defines quality time as, "time spent giving all of one's attention to someone." *All of one's attention* is worth repeating again because that means giving your undivided attention without any distractions in the background. In other words, this might mean you need to turn off the TV or put your cell phone away and engage in meaningful eye-to-eye contact by *really* being present in the moment. In the current pace in which this world runs, this definitely means *putting on the breaks* and slowing down. In doing this you are communicating that the other person you are with is special and greatly valued. To create a foundation for life-giving relationships, learning how to share your soul with someone whom you are safe with both emotionally and physically is the ultimate aim for the healthiest of relationships. You do that when someone cares enough about you to spend time with you by both valuing and validating your opinion—allowing you to feel heard and understood. *Undivided attention* with another equals *unconditional love*.

Tangible Takeaway

Use this Tangible Takeaway as a personal assessment and evaluate how you give another your undivided attention. Do you:

- Put your cell phone down when in conversation?
- Keep eye contact with another while in conversation?
- Listen attentively and engage in the conversation?
- Show empathy (have a nonjudgmental outlook)?
- Avoid distractions of any kind while in conversation?
- Are there any changes that need to be made?

If You're a Bird, I'm a Bird

Two people are better off than one,
for they can help each other succeed.
If one person falls, the other can reach out and help.
But someone who falls alone is in real trouble.

ECCLESIASTES 4:9–10 NLT

THE movie industry tugged at America's heart strings in the 2004 romantic drama *The Notebook.* Many have quoted lines from this Nicholas Sparks' novel-inspired movie. Heartfelt quotes such as Noah penned to Allie: "The best love is the kind that awakens the soul and makes us reach for more, that plants a fire in our hearts and brings peace to our minds." Or... "I am nothing special. But in one respect I have succeeded as gloriously as anyone who's ever lived: I've loved another with all my heart and soul; and to me, this has always been enough."[8] Therapeutically, perhaps, the most powerful quote of all is when Noah says to Allie, "If you're a bird, I'm a bird."

Its power rests in what it implies: *that if it is important to you, it is important to me...*and when you connect at that core level, you feel loved at the deepest level, which is an unconditional kind of love. It even parallels what Paul wrote in Scripture, "Rejoice with those who rejoice, weep with those who weep" (Romans 12:15 ESV). Spending time with someone, knowing them fully from the inside out, requires our undivided attention.

Tangible Takeaway

"If you're a bird, I'm a bird." —Noah, The Notebook

Our most important application is from our famous movie quote...if it is important to you, it is important to me. Ask yourself, what does this application mean to you in regard to a relationship that you are trying to nurture and grow ultimately into a bond of connection?

"We" Not "Me"

Behold, how good and how pleasant it is
for brothers to dwell together in unity!

PSALM 133:1 NASB

ANY winning coach will tell you that ultimately winning teams are made of players that learn how to have each other's back, learn how to sacrifice for their teammates, and learn how to work together as *one*...not as individual units. The same is true for any healthy relationship. If it is to remain healthy, each will learn the art of sacrifice, each will learn how to have the other's back, and the relationship will learn how to work things out *together*. Scripture even encourages us in Psalm 133:1 (NASB), "Behold, how good and how pleasant it is for brothers to dwell together in unity!" When one hurts, we all hurt. When one cries, we all cry. When one laughs, we all laugh. We need each other!

Jesus set the model for team and unity as He set the example for *one flesh* in marriage. Healthy marriages learn to live as *we* instead of a *me* and a *me*. Unhealthy marriages live as a *me* and a *me*. And a *me* and a *me* will never work when you are joined together as *one flesh*. God desires to be a player on our *we* team, helping us learn better how to validate and to become unified on decisions. The end result renders an unwavering trust between the two, producing an unprecedented, powerful team worth every effort.

Tangible Takeaway

Is this a new concept to you? Thinking of your marriage as we instead of a me and a me? Ask God to help you in the we-ness of your relationship as it relates to what "one flesh" means.

Celebrating Our Differences

Having gifts that differ according to the grace given to us,
let us use them: if prophecy, in proportion to our faith;
if service, in our serving; the one who teaches, in his
teaching; the one who exhorts, in his exhortation; the one
who contributes, in generosity; the one who leads, with
zeal; the one who does acts of mercy, with cheerfulness.

ROMANS 12:6—8 ESV

IN Scripture, we read about the life of two very different sisters who had one very important thing in common—their love for Jesus. Their names were Mary and Martha. Martha was the older sister of Mary, overtly identifying herself as having a superior gift of hospitality, who paid scrupulous attention to detail, with a desire to please and a need to serve. Luke 10:38 (ESV) reveals to us the gift of hospitality: "Now as they went on their way, Jesus entered a village. And a woman named Martha welcomed him into her house." In Martha's desperate need to please, prepare, serve, and be hospitable, she let distraction become the focus of the day. Preparation was the focus for Martha. Luke 10:40 (NASB) says, "But Martha was distracted with all her preparations...." Mary's disposition, on the other hand, was carefree, easygoing, and led by her heart. When Jesus and His disciples came for a visit, how does Mary respond? Luke 10:39 (ESV) says, "And she had a sister called Mary, who sat at the Lord's feet and listened to his teaching." Mary's focus was on one person and one person only: *Jesus*. Mary did not think of the traditions of the day with regard to hospitality or preparations because Jesus entered her home. *He and He alone captured her heart.* This dynamic between sisters caused a bit of turmoil to which Jesus replies in Luke 10:41-42 (NASB), "But the Lord answered and said to her, 'Martha, Martha, you are worried and bothered about so many things; but only one thing is necessary, for Mary has chosen the good part, which shall not be taken away from her.'" Notice Jesus did not say, "Martha, be like Mary." He said, "Mary has chosen what is better." This relationship model is for us to reflect upon as we celebrate our differences "according to the grace given to us."

Tangible Takeaway

Instead of viewing differences in relationships as a negative, how can you celebrate them as the gifts Christ has uniquely given?

Shaping and Sharpening

In the same way that iron sharpens iron,
a person sharpens the character of his friend.

PROVERBS 27:17 THE VOICE

THERE is a good chance that in all relationships there will come a time where differences of opinion will occur. The good news is that God can use these times to bring about our sharpening. Did you know that when iron is rubbed against another piece of iron, it shapes and sharpens it? And just like iron sharpens iron, relationships can be shaped and sharpened too. God longs for us to show more empathy to one another, to listen more intently to each other, and to live out His love in tangible ways. God wants us to access these avenues of action, concern, empathy, and listening to shape each other as we give Him access to do so through us each day. God is always shaping and sharpening us to become more like Him. To use a metaphor: the "rubbing process" at times may not "feel" so good during the time of "shaping" and "sharpening"...but the outcome—becoming an image-bearer of Christ—is priceless and worth it all!

Tangible Takeaway

Based off our devotional verse today, you influence those you come in contact with each day either in a positive or negative way. Spend some quality time with Jesus by reading through this prayer:

"God, I praise Your name first and foremost for who You are. I am in great need of Your confidence in me to do what only You can do. I pray that as iron sharpens iron, You will sharpen me, and that in turn You will speak through another to me and that I will hear through Your ears. Teach me, Jesus, what You would have me learn. I love You. Thank You for loving me."

Hold All Things Loosely

Set your minds on things that are above,
not on things that are on earth.

COLOSSIANS 3:2 ESV

HOLDING *all things loosely* feels like a modern-day translation of Colossians 3:2, doesn't it? When we *hold all things loosely*, it's our attempt as humans to follow Paul's call to loosen our grip on things of this earth while grabbing tightly to things above. At times that feels like walking on a tightrope—wobbling between hanging on too tightly to our earthly idols, yet trying with heartfelt sincerity to loosen those grips while looking to things above. God knows our struggle and does not want us to be enslaved or in bondage to anyone or anything on this earth—whether it be of material value, occupational status and gain, or even a relationship that has caused us to shift our eyes away from Him. Humans think we know all things, and we get our minds set on proving it.

Paul uses reverse psychology as he says to set our minds on things above, not on things on earth. Learning to live with an attitude of *holding all things loosely* helps keep everything in perspective. Healthy relationships look up before they look to each other. Do you *hold things loosely* so that God can be preeminent in your life? Is He first?

Tangible Takeaway

Read the following verses below.

- *"So we do not set our sights on the things we can see with our eyes. All of that is fleeting; it will eventually fade away. Instead, we focus on the things we cannot see, which live on and on"* (II Corinthians 4:18 The Voice).

- *"Seek first the kingdom of God and His righteousness, and then all these things will be given to you too"* (Matthew 6:33 The Voice).

How do these two verses apply to the phrase "holding all things loosely" in your life?

Child of God

*Consider the kind of extravagant love the Father
has lavished on us—He calls us children of God!
It's true; we are His beloved children.
And in the same way the world didn't recognize Him,
the world does not recognize us either.*

I JOHN 3:1 THE VOICE

EVERYONE searches to know who they are. While some search for their identities by taking personality quizzes, others rely on labels placed on them by their friends, parents, former teachers, etc. Have you ever heard someone say, "I'm a one?" Or..."I'm a seven?" Or on the flip side... have you ever had someone pin a number on you? If you have, you probably know they were referring to the Enneagram, a typology of nine interconnected personality types. You can take a test online to figure out if you are a #1 (The Reformer) or a #2 (The Helper)—all the way to #9 (The Peacemaker). The Enneagram challenge is "to discover our true selves in discovering God, and to find more of God in finding more of our true selves. As you discover yourself in a new way...you'll also find that you are paving the way to the wiser, more compassionate person you want to become."[9] The same is true in any given relationship. The more you discover yourself and who you are in your relationship with God, the more that relationship with God can be reflected in your relationship with another. God rejoices when this happens because He has an extravagant love that He lavishes on His children.

Tangible Takeaway

Before doing anything (like taking a test): First seek God... ask HIM who you are...He fearfully and wonderfully made you (Psalm 139:14). God knows you best. Then whatever number you find yourself on the Enneagram...invite God into that space and ask Him to grow you into the healthiest person you can be spiritually and emotionally.

Freedom from Pride

*A person's pride brings him down, but one of humble
spirit has a firm hold on honor and respect.*

PROVERBS 29:23 THE VOICE

THE opposite of pride is humility. In fact, the Merriam-Webster definition of humility is "freedom from pride or arrogance." Do you long for freedom? Staying humble in any relationship keeps tensions down and minds open. This happens because no one is dominating the relationship and allows freedom for God to work and the relationship to flourish. Does that sound renewing and refreshing? Yes...because it has the ability to restore your connection with another as a safe haven. Scripture reminds us that "wisdom accompanies those who are humble" (Proverbs 11:2 The Voice). Humility makes us teachable, allowing us to be quick to hear and slow to respond with greater intent at the proper time. God honors and exalts humility. He also detests the proud. "A person's pride brings him down, but one of humble spirit has a firm hold on honor and respect" (Proverbs 29:23 The Voice). Relationships that hold honor and respect as their anchor remain strong during the storm because they hold each other firm. God affirms the humble in spirit, and He is our help in attaining humility. He desires to come alongside us. "For everyone who exalts himself will be humbled, and he who humbles himself will be exalted" Luke 14:11 (ESV).

Tangible Takeaway

Take some time for yourself and truly search the Scriptures and your own heart as you look up these passages in God's Word that He has graciously given us as the guide to freedom from pride.

- *Proverbs 11:2*
- *Proverbs 16:18*
- *Proverbs 29:23*
- *Proverbs 8:13*
- *Proverbs 18:12*
- *Proverbs 16:5*
- *James 4:10*
- *Proverbs 22:4*
- *1 Peter 5:6*
- *Proverbs 15:33*

Learn to Laugh

*He will yet fill your mouth with laughter
and your lips with shouting.*

JOB 8:21 NASB

HEALTHY laughter acts like a sort of healing agent in almost *any* relationship...like salve to a wound...and should be *fun* and *uplifting*. The more you laugh, the more you connect. Learning how to laugh at yourself and with another in a *positive* way is a healthy way to enjoy each other. Laughter is contagious and draws people in. Laughter has the power to heal and is just plain fun. Laughter also does the body good! And, according to a recent article by the Mayo Clinic Staff, they agree that laughter is just what the doctor ordered. Laughter can:

- Stimulate many organs. Laughter enhances your intake of oxygen-rich air, stimulates your heart, lungs, and muscles, and increases the endorphins that are released by your brain.
- Activate and relieve your stress response. A rollicking laugh fires up and then cools down your stress response,

and it can increase your heart rate and blood pressure. The result? A good, relaxed feeling.

- Soothe tension. Laughter can also stimulate circulation and aid muscle relaxation, both of which can help reduce some of the physical symptoms of stress.
- Improve your immune system. Negative thoughts manifest into chemical reactions that can affect your body by bringing more stress into your system and decreasing your immunity. In contrast, positive thoughts can actually release neuropeptides that help fight stress and potentially more serious illnesses.
- Relieve pain. Laughter may ease pain by causing the body to produce its own natural painkillers.[10]

Tangible Takeaway

Laugh more...no, really...laugh more!

"Go ahead and give it a try. Turn the corners of your mouth up into a smile and then give a laugh, even if it feels a little forced. Once you've had your chuckle, take stock of how you're feeling. Are your muscles a little less tense? Do you feel more relaxed or buoyant? That's the natural wonder of laughing at work."

—Mayo Clinic Staff, Stress Management

*Our relationships
are as healthy as
we are individually.*

—SUSAN GOSS

Sweet and Healing

Pleasant words are a honeycomb,
sweet to the soul and healing to the bones.

PROVERBS 16:24 NASB

- I LOVE YOU.
- *I really appreciate you.*
- *You are beautiful.*
- *I am proud of you.*
- *You are awesome.*
- *Thank you.*
- *I respect you so much.*

Although each of these convey affirming words, the real definition of "words of affirmation" comes from the meaning behind each phrase. For example:

- *I love you because _____.*
- *I really appreciate you because _____.*
- *You are beautiful because _____.*
- *I am proud of you because _____.*
- *You are awesome because _____.*
- *Thank you because _____.*
- *I respect you so much because _____.*

The power of positive words is mentioned in Scripture... "Sweet to the soul and healing to the bones" (Proverbs 16:24 NASB). John Gottman from The Gottman Institute says, "The 'magic ratio' is 5 to 1. This means that for every negative interaction during conflict, a stable and happy marriage has five (or more) positive interactions."[11] Although Gottman's research was intended for marriages, this has been therapeutically used as a universal truth. In any relationship, it is wise to think of using five positives and/or words of affirmation to one negative.

Tangible Takeaway

Have you ever said anything just to fill air? Not really knowing what you are saying? Words are powerful. "Death and life are in the power of the tongue" (Proverbs 18:21 ESV). What we do doesn't necessarily back up our words. So think about the meaning behind your words and practice by filling in the blanks.

- I love you because _____.
- I really appreciate you because _____.
- You are beautiful because _____.
- I am proud of you because _____.
- You are awesome because _____.
- Thank you because _____.
- I respect you so much because _____.

I'm Sorry

> *Live in harmony with each other. Don't be*
> *too proud to enjoy the company of ordinary*
> *people. And don't think you know it all!*
>
> ROMANS 12:16 NLT

MOST relationships have been restored to complete health or completely severed by the use, or not, of two small but powerful words: *I'm sorry*. When what we have said or done has been the reason for a break in relationship and pride has kept us from having a repentant heart, we begin to give birth to a hardened heart. Pride can be dangerous. Let's look at some reasons why:

Merriam-Webster defines pride as "the quality or state of being proud: such as inordinate self-esteem: conceit."

Wikipedia defines pride as "a negative connotation referring to a foolishly and irrationally corrupt sense of one's personal value, status, or accomplishment."

Pride by its own definition hampers one's own ability to be able to accurately view one's own value without being overly conceited and judgmental toward another. In turn this can be destructive to building a healthy relationship and makes it more difficult to admit wrong. In Scripture we find Paul encouraging the church of Colossae, even while in prison, to show compassion and forgiveness toward one another. In Colossians 3:13–14 (NASB) he writes, "Bearing with one another, and forgiving each other, whoever has a complaint against anyone; just as the Lord forgave you, so also should you. Beyond all these things put on love, which is the perfect bond of unity." We can begin a language such as Paul admonished through his teachings and writings by the use of just two words...*I'm sorry*...and these words cannot be said if pride is present.

Tangible Takeaway

Only one question, but you have to process it and spend time with God for the answer: Is pride keeping you from saying I'm sorry?

Excuses, Excuses

*Therefore, if you are bringing an offering
to God and you remember that your brother
is angry at you or holds a grudge against you,
then leave your gift before the altar, go to your brother,
repent and forgive one another, be reconciled,
and then return to the altar to offer your gift to God.*

MATTHEW 5:23—24 THE VOICE

"I'M sorry *but*..." Did that sting? Someone just hurt you and then they come back with, "I'm sorry...(get ready for it)...*but*." Once the *but* is added, it negates the apology, doesn't it? To the one who has been hurt, it starts feeling more like an excuse rather than an apology. *Oh, the power of a genuine apology...a humble one without any excuses or rationalizations* because then the one who has been hurt feels validated that they have been wronged. Now someone is acknowledging that by saying I'm sorry...period...no buts...only *I'm sorry*. Saying "I'm sorry...*but*" is: #1 insincere and #2 like pointing a finger. Benjamin Franklin once said, "Never ruin an apology with an excuse." It is important to be ready with a sincere heart before you apologize because you do not know how the other person will receive it. We can only do our part.

Tangible Takeaway

Now read Psalm 51 in full and follow David's model of a sincere apology.

- *He showed sorrow.*
- *He owned up to his sin.*
- *He asked for forgiveness.*
- *He expressed desire to do right.*

Expectations

But as the Scriptures say,
"No eye has ever seen and no ear has ever heard
and it has never occurred to the human heart
all the things God prepared for those who love Him."

I CORINTHIANS 2:9 THE VOICE

WHEN something breaks down in your car, you take it to the shop with the expectation that it will soon be repaired. When you are in the mood for your favorite restaurant, you go with the expectation to leave full and satisfied. When we pray expectantly, we are anticipating God's work in our life. In all these cases, expectation is good. On the other hand, expectations can also wreak havoc on relationships when they are unrealistic, unspoken, and/or not mutually agreed upon. For example, when you realize you have an expectation that you didn't know was there until the behavior that was assumed went unmet. Case scenario:

Sally and Jake go for a date, and Sally has the expectation (because of her family of origin) that Jake will be a gentleman and open her car door because she has been taught that this represents to her that the gentleman respects her. This does not happen, and Sally begins to question Jake as to why...and conflict begins.

Expectations can be both good and bad. Scripture provides the ultimate example for expectancy into the Kingdom of God. Setting our expectations on the promises of God keeps our minds laser-focused and away from worldly distractions.

Tangible Takeaway

It is important that we realize and understand that expectations can be both good and bad. Give one example or scenario of each.

- Good _____
- Bad _____

It's My Pleasure

*So encourage each other and build
each other up, just as you are already doing.*

I THESSALONIANS 5:11 NLT

HAVE you ever been to Chick-fil-A®? They have heartfelt hospitality and are the quintessential cornerstone for customer service as it relates to encouraging the customer. President and COO, Dan Cathy, of Chick-fil-A is quoted saying, "The word 'restaurant' means place of restoration, and we think of Chick-fil-A as an oasis where people can be restored. We strive to treat people better than the place down the street. One way we do that is by remembering that we're all people with a lot of emotional things going on that don't necessarily show on the surface, so we try to offer amenities and kindness that minister to the heart."[12] One customer is known to have said, "When I am having a bad day, I like to drive-thru Chick-fil-A, and when I leave I always feel better about myself." Chick-fil-A made famous the phrase, "It's my pleasure," which makes anyone feel special. We can all learn a thing or two from Chick-fil-A.

Paul clearly states in I Thessalonians 5:11 that we are to "encourage each other and build each other up." The Merriam-Webster definition of encourage is to "inspire with courage, spirit, or hope." So many times we are *thinking* about how to encourage others, yet we do not say a word. Our intent is good, but we fail to execute. We verbally need to make the effort to not only *think* but also *speak* our words of encouragement. Let's take a lesson from Chick-fil-A to inspire others around us with courage, spirit, or hope.

Tangible Takeaway

Who can you impact in a positive way today? Set a daily goal to intentionally encourage those you come in contact with verbally. While shopping, at home, at work, or wherever the day takes you...be intentional. It truly will be your pleasure.

Dangerous Assumptions

You shall not testify falsely [that is, lie, withhold, or manipulate the truth] against your neighbor (any person).

EXODUS 20:16 AMP

ASSUMPTIONS can be dangerous in relationships because if a wrong assumption is made, then a lie is believed without validation about the truth. When the lie is believed, then you act on it, which becomes a "false testimony against your neighbor." This is a scenario that happens frequently in relationships. For example, it happens in a marriage when the spouses treat each other almost as enemies because they are assuming the worst of each other.

Checking our presumptions is a very simple yet powerful tool in helping fight against assumptions. When we stop and clarify, we get the truth. Stopping and clarifying sounds like this: "Is that true what you said? Am I correct?" This provides the opportunity for the other to respond to see if what was said was interpreted correctly or if it was misunderstood. Learning to replace assumptions with clarity and understanding brings peace and harmony to relationships. Scripture says it perfectly in Proverbs 17:27 (ESV), "Whoever restrains his words has knowledge, and he who has a cool spirit is a man of understanding." Ask God to have a *cool spirit* in and through you when you feel threatened to believe a *lie* and *withhold or manipulate the truth against your neighbor or any person.* With a *cool spirit* you can then stop and clarify to gain truth.

Tangible Takeaway ···

Is there a relationship in your life that needs to be repaired based off assumptions that have been made? Ask God to reveal and guide you in how to clarify any misunderstanding and to begin to repair. It is never too late.

True Emotions

*It is not what goes into the mouth
that defiles a person, but what comes out
of the mouth; this defiles a person.*

MATTHEW 15:11 ESV

*Let your speech always be gracious,
seasoned with salt, so that you may know
how you ought to answer each person.*

COLOSSIANS 4:6 ESV

DID you ever think that your radio in your car could be used as a relationship analogy? If you are looking at a radio, there is a volume knob that you can turn louder or softer or actually turn off and on. Just like a radio, we have a vast range of emotions. We can turn them off and on pretty easily, just like we can get louder or softer. Think of volume on a scale of 1 to 10...1 being super soft and 10 being super loud. When someone stays at a volume 10 for an extended period of time, they fade into white noise. Equally, if someone stays at a volume 1, they too fade into white noise. After a while you just don't hear them anymore. For instance, if someone is fearful of snakes and they scream at a volume 10 when they see one—that would make sense. However, if a small fly landed on the picnic table, you wouldn't expect a volume 10 reaction. The same is true in our relationships. We are not always at a volume 1 or at a volume 10 because the issues of our heart are not always the same. What is the volume on your knob today? Are you angry? Are you happy? Are you sad? Are you joyful? God is the creator of *all* emotions, and we want our volume to match our heart and our emotions. Using the illustration of the radio knob can greatly affect the way we convey our emotions to another so that they can receive it in the way it was intended.

Tangible Takeaway

Looking at the scale—do your emotions match what you are trying to convey to another?

Do Your Part

May the words of my mouth and the meditation of my heart
be pleasing to You, O LORD, my rock and my Redeemer.

PSALM 19:14 NLT

PSALM 19:14 is an example of a humbling prayer to recite each and every day. "May the words of my mouth and the meditation of my heart be pleasing to You, O LORD, my rock and my Redeemer." We are called to represent Jesus well. Although the ways to represent Jesus might be infinite, we as humans sometimes get bogged down trying to figure out or even control the who, what, when, where, and how of that tangible manifestation and can quickly become defeated. Jesus illustrated with extraordinary wisdom both His creativity and our deep desire to represent Him well in one particular parable: Matthew 25:35–40 (NASB), " 'For I was hungry, and you gave Me something to eat; I was thirsty, and you gave Me something to drink; I was a stranger, and you invited Me in; naked, and you clothed Me; I was sick, and you visited Me; I was in prison, and you came to Me.' Then the righteous will answer Him,

'Lord, when did we see You hungry, and feed You, or thirsty, and give You something to drink? And when did we see You a stranger, and invite You in, or naked, and clothe You? When did we see You sick, or in prison, and come to You?' The King will answer and say to them, 'Truly I say to you, to the extent that you did it to one of these brothers of Mine, even the least of them, you did it to Me.'" The lesson here is to *be the hands and feet of Jesus* in whatever capacity we find ourselves. Whether it is working with disaster relief, World Vision, a local nonprofit, a homeless shelter, a food pantry, a women's or children's shelter, volunteering for ministry at church, visiting the homebound, or helping a friend in need, there are endless opportunities. Ask God to direct you where He wants you to serve so that He can do and be creative in and through you.

Tangible Takeaway

Do your part and pray Psalm 19:14, "May the words of my mouth and the meditation of my heart be pleasing to You, O Lord, my rock and my Redeemer."

Do as I Have Done to You

I have given you an example to follow. Do as I have done to you.

JOHN 13:15 NLT

WHAT makes a good leader? The answer to that question would largely be based off of one's personal experience... both good and bad. Leadership is modeled throughout Scripture, but never more beautifully or intimately displayed than in John 13 when Jesus gathers His disciples for supper the night before His death. After they ate, Jesus "got up from supper, and laid aside His garments; and taking a towel, He girded Himself. Then He poured water into the basin, and began to wash the disciples' feet and to wipe them with the towel with which He was girded" (John 13:4–5 NASB). One can only imagine what was going on in the disciples' minds—some shocked, some embarrassed for Jesus to wash the dirtiest part of them. Nevertheless, Jesus began making His way around the table one at a time, gently washing his disciples' feet, and acting more like a servant than the Son of Man.

Jesus led by example, but more than that, Jesus was

saying to His followers, "You, My beloved disciples, are to become My exact counterpart...an extension of Me when I am gone. Do as you have seen Me do." In John 13:15, Jesus says, "I have given you an example to follow. Do as I have done to you." There was no pride in washing feet. Jesus beautifully modeled humility with authority, seeking first His Father rather than going "rogue." Jesus was saying to His disciples and to us today...*if you want to represent Me well, if you want to be a strong leader whom others should follow, then there can be no thirst for power, presence of pride, or motivation of greed.* Erwin McManus expresses this thought extremely well in his book *Uprising* as he writes, "If we push ourselves to the top, we are pushing ourselves away from the presence of God. When we move ourselves to the place of servanthood, we join God in His eternal purpose. When we serve others, we look strangely like God. God stands alone as Creator and Redeemer...He stands there also as servant."[13]

Tangible Takeaway

A heart of humility is revealed and wisdom beams when we open ourselves up for growth both in leadership and in life. How do you lead? How do you serve others? Are you an image bearer of Jesus? Jesus was our example, and we should strive to do as He did to us.

The Prize

Do you not know that those who run in a
race all run, but only one receives the prize?
Run in such a way that you may win.
I CORINTHIANS 9:24 NASB

IN 1992, British athlete Derek Redmond was set for the race of his life in the 400-meter semifinals at the Barcelona Olympics. In lane five, Derek had a great start out of the blocks, running with the focus of being the winner as he crossed the finish line. But then something happened: a deafening pop. Derek's body began to fade into the track as he tightly grabbed hold of his hamstring. Officials started moving toward him. One by one, he waved them away as he began hobbling around the track to the finish line with the same focus as he started the race. Then a familiar touch and a voice made the difference. "Derek it's me. You don't need to do this." "It was my dad," Derek said in an interview. "I had held it together until I heard his voice, and when I knew it was my dad, I lost it. This man has been alongside me my whole life...supporting me... and when I heard his voice, I knew I could let down."

His dad said, "You're a champion; you've got nothing to prove." "Dad, I want to finish, get me back in the semi-final," Derek said in that moment. His dad replied, "Okay. We started this thing together, and now we'll finish it together." Derek and his dad together crossed the finish line in the world's greatest competition.[14]

Sometimes it's about so much more than the competition itself, isn't it? All the hours, the years of training, the regimen, the laser focus, and the sacrifices he and others made along the way. Jesus understands discipline, competition, and sacrifice—all the way to the cross! We must run to win. Not vicariously living through others crossing the finish line, but wanting Jesus more than we want life because that's exactly what He did for us! We're meant to "train" vigorously, diligently, and purposefully. We must run in such a way as to "get the prize" because when life throws in a curve ball and we find ourselves curled up in a ball of pain in whatever form "pain" may take, like Derek, we can get back up and finish the race.

Tangible Takeaway ·······························

Derek's dad was right when he said we have nothing to prove. And just like Derek, we need to learn to lean on Jesus. Are you leaning on Jesus?

*And let us consider
how to stir up one another
to love and good works,
not neglecting to meet together,
as is the habit of some,
but encouraging one another.*

HEBREWS 10:24–25 ESV

Content Versus Process

A soft answer turns away wrath,
but a harsh word stirs up anger.

PROVERBS 15:1 ESV

HAS anyone ever told you, "It's not what you say...it's how you say it"? What we say is the *content.* How we say it is the *process.* If *content* is important, then *process* is essential. How we say what we say is critical to the message for the message to be received accurately. Two people may say the same thing, but it can be interpreted two totally different ways. For example, someone says, "I like your new haircut" while smiling and with sincerity. This is easily taken as a compliment. Or someone says, "I like your new haircut" while shaking their head and rolling their eyes...this is instantly taken as an insult.

We find this even in Scripture with Jesus and the Pharisees. At times both are delivering the same truth but in two totally different ways. Jesus lovingly and with tender care explains the Scriptures, walks side by side, eating and having fellowship with those He came in contact with in order to build relationship and further the Kingdom, and allowing those He is with to ask questions and engage in conversation. The Pharisees, on the other hand, were a religious group of highly intelligent men who knew every letter of the Jewish law. The Pharisees took a one-up approach and spoke down to others and left out the relational piece. They gave rules and regulations. Their message (content) might be the *same*, however, the delivery completely opposite...leaving the hearer void of connection between head and heart. Where Jesus valued the process, which is connection, the Pharisees valued the rules and regulations, which is content.

Tangible Takeaway

Practice reading this statement in two different voices— one soft and the other harsh.

Are you on your way home?

Remember—content is important but process is essential.

Guard Your Heart

Guard your heart above all else,
for it determines the course of your life.

PROVERBS 4:23 NLT

GUARD your heart is a phrase that is easily said...but what does it actually mean? Scripture plainly teaches us to, "Guard your heart above all else, for it determines the course of your life." If we are advised to guard our heart above all else, then our heart must be of great *value* and should be *treasured.* This is essential because whatever we let in our heart will eventually come out. Hosea 11:7 (The Voice) speaks to the matter of our inner human nature: "My people are determined to turn away from Me." We have to combat our sinful nature by turning *toward* God and praying Romans 8:27 (NASB): "and He who searches the hearts knows what the mind of the Spirit is, because He intercedes for the saints according to the will of God." Just like the heart keeps the physical body alive by pumping blood and supplying oxygen to give life, so, too, is the heart the great influencer in every other part of life—both spiritually and emotionally. Paul leads us to the answer of "how to guard the gift of the heart" in Philippians 4:6–7 (ESV) when he says, "Do not be anxious about anything, but in everything by prayer and supplication with thanksgiving let your requests be made known to God. And the peace of God, which surpasses all understanding, *will guard your hearts* and your minds in Christ *Jesus*." Guarding the heart first begins by spending time *with God*. God desires to bring peace to our hearts and minds and, when this happens, *from it "flow" the springs of life (Proverbs 4:23)*, which will be reflected in other relationships.

Tangible Takeaway ....

Think about your heart. Do you guard it well according to Paul in Philippians 4:6–7? Pray out loud each Scripture in today's devotional. Be intentional by going toward God. It is a daily choice—what will you choose?

First Love

But I have this [charge] against you,
that you have left your first love
[you have lost the depth of love
that you first had for Me].

REVELATION 2:4 AMP

WE tend to make everything about us, and when we do, everything tends to go south. When we are in a difficult relationship and think we know the cause, we fix it. Why? Because we are capable people. But God has a different way. His way is about Him. He wants us to look up. "But first and most importantly seek (aim at, strive after) His kingdom and His righteousness [His way of doing and being right—the attitude and character of God], and all these things will be given to you also" (Matthew 6:33 AMP). God wants to be our first love and the One we call out to even before we look to each other. When we look to each other first, we immediately become dependent on a person rather than God for wisdom. However, dependence on

God's wisdom gives us strength and guidance in our relationships. And dependence on God steers us back on track. Going to God first is a disciplined practice; as you do, He gets bigger in your life.

Tangible Takeaway

Have you left your first love?

When you run into a problem, whom do you run to first?

When you are in a difficult relationship, do you focus on God first? Or do you focus only on the problem at hand?

Mirror Moment

Explore me, O God, and know the real me.
Dig deeply and discover who I am.
Put me to the test and watch
how I handle the strain. Examine me
to see if there is an evil bone in me,
and guide me down Your path forever.

PSALM 139:23—24 THE VOICE

PHYSICALLY—what do you see when you look in the mirror? On the surface, we only see a reflection of ourselves. Spiritually—what do you see when you look in your heart? Mirror moments with God are a reflection of our hearts according to Him. As we look in the mirror, we see ourselves. In mirror moments with God, we're asking God to reflect what He sees in us. Psalm 139:4 (NLT) says, "You know what I am going to say even before I say it, LORD." Which implies we can be completely transparent before God. We can't shock Him, surprise Him, or snow Him. We can be honest in our time with God. We cleanse our heart during our mirror moments with God by releasing to Him all of our unforgiveness and shame so that we do not carry unnecessary baggage into our relationships. Mirror moments with God help reflect His heart in ours.

Tangible Takeaway ....

Be completely transparent and honest in your mirror moment with God about any shame identity, such as: "God, is it true that I am not good enough? Is it true that I am less than? Is it true that I am worthless? God, examine and explore the real me. Help me know the real me as You see me." Psalm 139:14 (NASB) says, "I will give thanks to You, for I am fearfully and wonderfully made; wonderful are Your works, and my soul knows it very well." Remind yourself of God's truth—that you are fearfully and wonderfully made. You are enough! You are loved! "How precious also are Your thoughts to me, O God! How vast is the sum of them! If I should count them, they would outnumber the sand. When I awake, I am still with You" (Psalm 139:17–18 NASB).

Look for the Good and You Will Find It

Those who seek good find the goodwill of others.
PROVERBS 11:27 THE VOICE

IT'S TRUE! If you are looking for the good even with only a glimmer of hope, you will find it. And let's be real, people just like to be around other people that are great at looking for the good because whether the good is grand and obvious or the good is only a glimmer of hope, they find it everywhere. Why? Because they intentionally look for it. And we are even encouraged in Scripture to do the same: "Those who seek good find the goodwill of others." Finding the good can change perspective.

A technique frequently used in therapy to help aid in the process of perspective-changing is known as *reframing* (also known as cognitive reframing), and therapists use this technique in order to help clients look at situations, people, or relationships in a different light. Positive reframing *is a technique to help view the other person's motives and behavior in a more* positive *light.* For example:

When a husband pursues a wife, sometimes it appears to be *nagging* to the wife, but with the use of a *positive reframe* it can be turned into a loving connection. As the wife begins to see the motive behind the behavior, the husband must slow the process down and allow his wife to know how much he values her. The wife then begins to experience her husband in a more positive way, seeing him as *good* and *loving* instead of pursuing and nagging.

The bad is so easy to spot and quick to call out. Let's do something countercultural and be different—*let's go for the positive reframe by looking for the good...and finding it!*

Tangible Takeaway

Think back on a recently encountered scenario of your own that might need a reframe in order to change the outcome to a more positive light. Ask yourself, "Did you look for the good in that scenario as our Scripture reminds us?"

Look for the Bad and It Will Find You

But those who look for evil
are sure to find it.

PROVERBS 11:27 THE VOICE

THE Pharisees set a gold standard for looking for the bad and finding it—in just about anyone and anything! For example, the Pharisees saw Jesus and the disciples eating at the table with many tax collectors and sinners. Immediately, the Pharisees began to question the disciples about why Jesus would be eating with such people. The Pharisees were only concerned with *who* Jesus was with because they were focused on the ceremonial practices and not caring about the heart. "But when Jesus heard this, He said, 'It is not those who are healthy who need a physician, but those who are sick. But go and learn what this means: "I desire compassion, and not sacrifice," for I did not come to call the righteous, but the sinners' " (Matthew 9:12–13 NASB). It is all about perspective—in

God's eyes, everyone is welcome at the table. "Those who seek good find the goodwill of others..." From the eyes of man, only a select few are invited. "But those who look for evil are sure to find it" (Proverbs 11:27 The Voice).

Tangible Takeaway

"It is not those who are healthy who need a physician, but those who are sick" (Matthew 9:12 NASB).

Do you see from the eyes of God or the eyes of man? Start by seeking the good to find the goodwill of others. Who can you invite to the table that is different than you that you normally don't find yourself sitting with? Begin there and ask God to see them with His eyes. Look for the good, and you will find it!

Attitude Is Everything

Do everything without complaining
and arguing, so that no one can criticize you.
Live clean, innocent lives as children of God,
shining like bright lights in a world
full of crooked and perverse people.

PHILIPPIANS 2:14—15 NLT

CHARLES Swindoll's famous quote on attitude wisely states, "I am convinced that life is 10 percent what happens to me and 90 percent of how I react to it. And so it is with you...we are in charge of our attitudes." Scripture's counterpart to this statement is Psalm 118:24 (ESV), "This is the day that the LORD has made; let us rejoice and be glad in it." This verse is not based on circumstance but on a daily decision to surrender our attitude to the Lord. *We are in charge of our attitudes.* We can both dwell on our difficult circumstance and *complain* or, as the Scripture says, *argue.* Or when the going gets tough, we can claim the promise God has given us in

Psalm 118:24, knowing it will not always be easy. But by personalizing the verse, God changes the heart which changes the attitude. We need to ask God to say Psalm 118:24 through us each and every day: "This is the day the Lord has made...I WILL rejoice and be glad in it."

Tangible Takeaway

We are in charge of our attitudes. Will you choose to dwell or claim the promise God has given us today? Remember, our attitude is not based upon our circumstances. Read aloud and ask God to say Psalm 118:24 in and through you. "This is the day the Lord has made...I WILL rejoice and be glad in it." Or you can go a step further and commit to memorizing this Scripture and reciting it daily as an attitude reminder.

Prayer: Ask

But he must ask in faith without any doubting,
for the one who doubts is like the surf of the sea,
driven and tossed by the wind.
For that man ought not to expect
that he will receive anything from the Lord,
being a double-minded man, unstable in all his ways.

JAMES 1:6—8 NASB

ONE interpretation of our devotional verse today would be: *pray like you mean it!* In other words, don't just do lip service to the relationship; actively pray for the relationship. God desires to be intimately involved in all your relationships. Every. Single. One. Have you asked God to see your spouse, child, parent, friend or coworker through His eyes? He loves them more than you do. Have you prayed and asked God to help them see you as He sees you? *Prayer changes relationships when we are praying with a faith that it will.* Prayer not only changes perspectives as God allows you to see what He sees, but it also changes hearts. God is able to provide wisdom in making good decisions as we become dependent on Him and less on ourselves. When we go it alone, we tend to mess things up. Have you ever experienced that? But Luke offers hope as he reminds us that we *ought always to pray and not lose heart (Luke 18:1).* Relationships can be beautiful and life-giving, but real life reveals that they can also be ugly and hard. We desperately need God's wisdom.

Tangible Takeaway

Prayer changes relationships when we are praying with a faith that it will.

Pray like you mean it.

Have you asked God to see your spouse, child, parent, friend, or coworker through His eyes?

Have you prayed and asked God to help them see you as He sees you?

Prayer: Trust

"You don't have enough faith," Jesus told them.
"I tell you the truth, if you had faith even
as small as a mustard seed, you could say
to this mountain, 'Move from here to there,'
and it would move. Nothing would be impossible."

MATTHEW 17:20 NLT

A therapeutic term used in counseling a lot is: "trust the process." It's hard sometimes to do because everyone wants immediate results. At times it does seem laborious going through the process, but every step helps gain more understanding and is imperative for the journey of healing and recovery. But because we live in a "microwave world" where everything is zapped and shortcuts are preferred, it is very difficult to sit still and wait for things to simmer. God asks us to wait and let things simmer while He is working, when we pray and ask Him to intervene in our lives and to work in our relationships. He asks us to *learn to trust in the process* of allowing Him to do *His thing* in the areas of our lives and relationships that we have asked Him to work and move in. God always has our back. He always knows best. Look to these words of guidance and encouragement from Proverbs 3:5–6 (NLT): "Trust in the LORD with all your heart; do not depend on your own understanding. Seek His will in all you do, and He will show you which path to take."

Tangible Takeaway

Is your faith as small as a mustard seed (Matthew 17:20)? Are you trusting God in your relationships? If so, ask Him to intervene.

Now, based on Proverbs 3:5–6, ask yourself these questions:

- *Are you trusting in the Lord with all your heart?*
- *Are you not depending on your own understanding?*
- *Are you seeking His will in all you do?*
- *Are you asking Him to show you which path to take?*

Prayer: Give Thanks

Rejoice always; pray without ceasing;
in everything give thanks; for this
is God's will for you in Christ Jesus.

I THESSALONIANS 5:16—18 NASB

ARE you thankful for the child God has placed in your life...whether a son or daughter, niece or nephew, neighbor, friend, or maybe even a student you are teaching? Has the word *thankful* run through your mind when you think of that particular child? Are you thankful for your spouse (if you are married), or perhaps a fiancé, siblings, parents, friends, coworkers... and the list goes on! Has the word *thankful* run through your mind when you think of any of these relationships? Paul admonishes us in I Thessalonians to give thanks in all things. When we allow our heart to be moved by God, we can then experience genuine thankfulness, not just lip service with empty words coming from the head, not the heart. When we ask God to intervene in our lives and in our relationships and trust Him to do so, Paul encourages us to thank God for what He *will* do. Thankfulness is a matter of the heart and causes us to have an attitude full of gratitude, connecting us in healthy relationships.

Tangible Takeaway ··

Genuine thankfulness comes from the heart. Lip service with empty words comes from the head. Where does your thankfulness come from? Using today's Scripture, make I Thessalonians 5:16–18, make a very personal prayer by adding your name in each blank below.

- _____ *(your name)* _____ *rejoice always;*
- _____ *(your name)* _____ *pray without ceasing;*
- _____ *(your name)* _____ *in everything give thanks;*
- *for this is God's will for* _____ *(your name)* _____ *in Christ Jesus.*

That "magic ratio" is 5 to 1.
This means that for every
negative interaction during conflict,
a stable and happy marriage has
five (or more) positive interactions.

—JOHN GOTTMAN,
The Magic Relationship Ratio, The Gottman Institute

Unswerving Allegiance

Then Jonathan made a covenant with David
because he loved him as himself.
Jonathan stripped himself of the robe that was
on him and gave it to David, with his armor,
including his sword and his bow and his belt.

I SAMUEL 18:3—4 NASB

MERRIAM-WEBSTER'S definition of *loyal* is: "unswerving in allegiance." Jonathan chose loyalty to God by giving up his rightful position as heir to the throne by stripping himself of his robe and armor including his sword, bow, and belt—and willingly giving them to David, the promised King of Israel. Because Jonathan was loyal to God first, he could then be loyal without jealousy in his friendship with David to fulfill God's promise. It is such a gift to have a loyal friend. One that you can count on through thick and thin, who is always there for you and has your back, knows you during the good times and the bad yet never stops loving you. God models that through unconditional love. Loyal friends tell you things you don't want to hear because they want the best for you. Sometimes they see things that you can't see, like an outsider looking in. A loyal, trustworthy friend is a gift from God.

Tangible Takeaway

What Jonathan did was unnatural. It is not our nature to give up an inheritance to the throne, but he willingly did because He was in tune to the will of God. Jonathan was loyal to God first so that he could be loyal to David's calling and encourage him along the way. Are you loyal to God first so that you can be loyal to others without attaching any unwanted emotional restrictions?

Families of Origin

God decided in advance to adopt us into His own family
by bringing us to Himself through Jesus Christ. This is
what He wanted to do, and it gave Him great pleasure.

EPHESIANS 1:5 NLT

SIBLING rivalry, parent-child conflict, rebellion, lack of independence, too controlling or no control at all, manipulation, divorce, functional or dysfunctional family? We are all a product or a part of how we were raised. All families are dysfunctional at some level in their own unique way, and we are not alone. There is no "perfect" family.

Dysfunctional families have been around from the beginning of time, starting in the Garden when God asked Adam where he was and he immediately pointed his finger to Eve and said, "It was she! The woman You gave me as a companion put the fruit in my hands, and I ate it" (Genesis 3:12 The Voice). Thus, the blaming begins. Jacob, Esau, and Rebekah provide us with another example of family dysfunction where we have a mother plotting with her son, against her husband, to steal the birthright from the firstborn son. Now that is dysfunction. To continue...a story of two brothers named Cain and Abel, where Cain's jealous heart would make him kill Abel because God preferred Abel's offering over his. The list goes on and on.

Families of origin begin with God. He is the creator of everything, and He desires to create patterns in our lives that honor Him and His people. Thank Him for the strengths, joys, and accomplishments in your families of origin. Equally, let go of the frustrations, resentments, and baggage of your family of origin and allow God to work because He doesn't see the dysfunction as we see it.

Tangible Takeaway ....

Pray this prayer over your family:

Lord, thank You for loving _____ (fill in the blank with each of your family members) . Help me release to You what I cannot control and handle in my family because I know You love them even more than I do. You are perfect and Your ways are perfect, and I trust in that. Thank You, Lord.

Genuine Happiness

Let love be genuine.

ROMANS 12:9 ESV

GOD found compassion on the people of Nineveh (a great city full of wicked people who were serving false gods). He asked Jonah to go to Nineveh and let the people know that if they didn't stop their ways, they would all be destroyed. However, Jonah didn't want to warn the people. He didn't think they deserved to be saved, so he disobeyed and took a boat to Tarshish and eventually found himself in the belly of a whale. Jonah was a disobedient prophet who did not want to do what God had called him to do. He was quick to judge others while neglecting to examine his own heart. God's love for Nineveh was through rejoicing in the repentance of 120,000 people, but Jonah was too fixated on himself to experience genuine happiness for them. God cared about the people, but Jonah cared only about himself. Have you ever been in Jonah's shoes, unable to experience genuine happiness for others because you were in the way? Sound familiar to anyone? We all have been there before and for reasons we wouldn't care to admit. Reasons such as pride, jealousy, comparison, and self-pity. *But genuine happiness calls us to think beyond ourselves and to invite God into the process of changing our hearts* because...*genuine happiness comes from a place of pure love, and love is genuine.*

Tangible Takeaway

Prepare your heart for the Tangible Takeaway by reading these verses out loud, then sit with God and ask the question that follows:

- *The purpose of my instruction is that all believers would be filled with love that comes from a pure heart, a clear conscience, and genuine faith (1 Timothy 1:5 NLT).*
- *Let love be genuine (Romans 12:9 ESV).*

Are you genuinely happy when others succeed, or is Jonah's story too close to home? If so, ask God why.

Creative and Memorable

*Therefore a man shall leave his father
and his mother and hold fast to his wife,
and they shall become one flesh.*

GENESIS 2:24 ESV

IF you have ever been to a wedding, then you might agree that the union of *two becoming one* is, without a doubt, historically one of the most beautiful and powerful ceremonies ever established in all of human history, as it represents *one flesh*.

Jesus' first miracle was at a wedding. Traditionally, Jewish weddings lasted a full seven days, and the bride's and groom's families provided the food and wine for everyone. But in the middle of this particular celebration *the wine ran out*. This meant that if the guests caught wind that the wine ran out, culturally speaking, it implied that the bride's and groom's families either did not care enough about their guests or did not have the appropriate funds to supply as much wine as desired. Mary, the mother of Jesus, sees the situation and turns to her Son for help.

Now there were six stone water jars there for the Jewish rites of purification, each holding twenty or thirty gallons. Jesus said to the servants, "Fill the jars with water." And they filled them up to the brim. And he said to them, "Now draw some out and take it to the master of the feast." So they took it. When the master of the feast tasted the water now become wine, and did not know where it came from (though the servants who had drawn the water knew), the master of the feast called the bridegroom and said to him, "...You have kept the the good wine until now" (John 2:6–10 ESV).

If Jesus can change water into wine, what have you asked Him to do in your life and relationships? If Jesus saved the bride's and groom's families from embarrassment and shame by not only doing the impossible but also by doing something creative and memorable, then why not consider asking God to do something creative and memorable in you?

Tangible Takeaway

Are you allowing God to show up big in your life?

Fully Known

O LORD, You have searched me and known me. You know
when I sit down and when I rise up; You understand
my thought from afar. You scrutinize my path and my
lying down, and are intimately acquainted with all
my ways. Even before there is a word on my tongue,
behold, O LORD, You know it all. You have enclosed me
behind and before, and laid Your hand upon me.

PSALM 139:1—5 NASB

IN the above Scripture, David expressed his understanding that God fully knew him and that nothing could be hidden from God. He was in awe of God's omniscience (being all-knowing) and omnipresence (being everywhere at the same time). Human relationships can be very fickle...here today...gone tomorrow. God is nothing like humans...absolutely nothing! Scripture even says that God is the same yesterday, today, and tomorrow (Hebrews 13:8). He is a solid rock. God is always safe. Scripture tells us that God knows what is on our tongue before we say it, which implies total honesty before Him. It's true, earthly relationships may come and go, but there is no place that you can go that God is not already there. "Where can I go from Your Spirit? Or where can I flee from Your presence? If I ascend to heaven, You are there; If I make my bed in Sheol, behold, You are there. If I take the wings of the dawn, if I dwell in the remotest part of the sea, even there Your hand will lead me and Your right hand will lay hold of me" (Psalm 139:7–10 NASB). At times, a human's love is calculated and finite, but God's love is forever and infinite. "How precious also are Your thoughts to me, O God! How vast is the sum of them! If I should count them, they would outnumber the sand. When I awake, I am still with You" (Psalm 139:17–18 NASB). Friend—you are never alone— AND you are fully known.

Tangible Takeaway

Turn Psalm 139:1–5 into a personal prayer:

O Lord, thank You for knowing me. You know when I sit down and when I rise up; You understand my thought from afar. You scrutinize my path and my lying down, and are intimately acquainted with all my ways. Even before there is a word on my tongue, behold, O Lord, You know it all. You have enclosed me behind and before, and laid Your hand upon me. Thank You, Jesus, for knowing me inside and out—and still loving me. Thank You for being my rock and for never leaving me. Amen.

The Prodigal Son

So he got up and came to his father.
But while he was still a long way off,
his father saw him and felt compassion for him,
and ran and embraced him and kissed him.

LUKE 15:20 NASB

THE story of the Prodigal Son is one of the most familiar parables found in Scripture.

"Once there was this man who had two sons. One day the younger son came to his father and said, 'Father, eventually I'm going to inherit my share of your estate. Rather than waiting until you die, I want you to give me my share now.' And so the father liquidated assets and divided them" (Luke 15:11–12 The Voice). The younger son would take it and go on his way where he "squandered his estate with loose living" (Luke 15:13 NASB). He acted foolishly and ended up losing absolutely everything and would "have gladly filled his stomach with the pods that the swine were eating" because "no one was giving anything to him'" (Luke 15:16 NASB).

Eventually, he would come back to his senses and return

to his father's house. What is beautiful is that his father never stopped looking for him. In fact, today's Scripture reads that "while he was still a long way off, his father saw him...and ran and embraced him and kissed him." Just like the father never stopped looking for his son to return home, Jesus never stops looking for us! Because of His unconditional love, He is constantly calling us to return home and is eagerly waiting to embrace us if we choose to turn back to Him.

Tangible Takeaway

Healthy relationships never stop looking or loving. They always hope and are ready twenty-four seven to give a warm embrace. Can you relate to the prodigal son or know someone who can? Can you relate to the father's waiting or know someone who is currently waiting for their prodigal son to return home? Don't give up hope because our Heavenly Father never stops looking for us and His love for us is unconditional.

Jesus Is Always Pursuing You

And he said to him, "Son, you have always been with me, and all that is mine is yours. But we had to celebrate and rejoice, for this brother of yours was dead and has begun to live, and was lost and has been found."

LUKE 15:31—32 NASB

THE parable of the Prodigal Son ends with the older son returning from the field to hear music and dancing coming from the house. The older son began questioning a servant what the celebration was for. The servant informed him that his brother had returned home safe and sound, so his father killed the fattened calf to celebrate. Hearing this news the older son "became angry and was not willing to go in; and his father came out and began pleading with him" (Luke 15:28 NASB). He went on to tell his father, "Look! For so many years I have been serving you and I have never neglected a command of yours; and yet you have never given me a young goat, so that I might celebrate with my friends" (Luke 15:29 NASB). Jesus used the older son in the parable to symbolize the

Pharisees who were self-righteous and sought to be affirmed and noticed for their works. When the father saw the prodigal son returning home, he immediately went to him. The father, in fact, was ready to receive both sons—the prodigal who left home and the older son who never left his side. The father leaves the celebration and pleads with his older son by saying, "Son, you have always been with me, and all that is mine is yours. But we had to celebrate and rejoice, for this brother of yours was dead and has begun to live, and was lost and has been found." Just like the father—whether you're the wayward prodigal son or the jealous, indignant older brother—Jesus is always pursuing you and is standing ready to receive you with a warm embrace.

Tangible Takeaway

Did you catch that? He wants both the prodigal son and the older brother. Just like the father never stopped looking for his son to return home and went to plead with his older son to join the celebration, Jesus never stops looking for or longing for us. No matter what we say or do, He never stops loving us. Can you say the same about your relationships? Are you looking, longing, and loving? Ask God...because it's never too late to start.

Sacrificial Friendship

Greater love has no one than this, that one
lay down his life for his friends.

JOHN 15:13 NASB

JESUS was the ultimate example of sacrificial friendship for each of us—all the way to the cross. He willingly gave up His life so that we could gain life in Him. Jesus' sacrifice is the foundation of our faith. Without Jesus laying down his life for his friends (us) we would have no hope (John 15:13). In fact, we are friends of His: "I have called you friends" (John 15:15 ESV). So what is friendship without sacrifice? If Jesus modeled sacrifice in friendship, shouldn't we?

In Scripture we find another example of sacrificial friendship through Jonathan and David. Both were true friends bound together by their relationships with God. "Jonathan loved him as himself" (I Samuel 18:1 NASB). However, there was a problem: Jonathan's father, King Saul, *hated* David and sought to kill him. Jonathan would put his life at risk and jeopardize his relationship with his own father by showing his commitment to David because he knew God's plan was for David to ascend to the throne, not himself as culture would have it. Jonathan's ultimate commitment was to God, not to tradition or culture. And David was committed to being obedient to his Lord. Both friends pointed the other toward God and away from pride.

Pointing your friend to God instead of to each other is such a valuable lesson to take from the friendship of Jonathan and David. Even when one has to sacrifice a "rightful place of privilege" because you know God has chosen your friend instead of you. Or current-day example: your friend gets the job and you don't. Have you invited God into the *easy* and the *hard* of your friendships?

Tangible Takeaway

Have you ever had a friend sacrifice for you like Jonathan and David? Or have you ever sacrificed for a friend like Jonathan and David? Are you overwhelmed with joy for Jesus' sacrifice for you? We can learn from Scripture that sacrifice is an underlying core principle of friendship. How can you lay down your life for your friends today?

I'm Done

He only is my rock and my salvation,
My stronghold; I shall not be shaken.

PSALM 62:6 NASB

HAVE you ever thought "I'm done" in regard to an unhealthy or even unwanted relationship or a particularly bad day? Have you ever thought that saying "I'm done" is a good thing? God loves it because then He can say, "Good, finally *you* are done...now let *Me* take over." He wants us to lay down our "I'm done" moments at His feet by pouring "out your heart to Him" (Psalm 62:8 NLT). By releasing our "I'm done" moments to God, we can be totally honest with God because He wants us to be.

Scripture beautifully reminds us that the Lord searches and knows us, understands our thoughts, is intimately acquainted with all our ways, and before we speak He knows it all (Psalm 139:1–4). We can confidently be honest with God because He already knows it all and still loves us unconditionally. In Him we have stability because "Jesus Christ is the same yesterday and today and forever" (Hebrews 13:8 NASB). He is a *solid rock* that *cannot be shaken*. When we are experiencing an "I'm done" moment, we need to honestly say, "God, I'm done. But You are not. I can't do this anymore, but You can. Work in and through me." Allow Him to work in that difficult relationship, in the days you don't want to get out of bed or to handle the bad news that is weighing you down. God. Is. Never. Done.

Tangible Takeaway

Rest in these facts today:

- *God is a solid rock that cannot be shaken. (Psalm 62:6)*
- *God knows it all and still loves you unconditionally. (Psalm 139:1–4)*
- *God is the same...yesterday, today, and forever. (Hebrews 13:8)*
- *You may be thinking "I'm done," but He is not. Release those moments to God and allow Him to do what only He can do in and through you.*

Count To Seven

Be still in the presence of the LORD,
and wait patiently for Him to act.
Don't worry about evil people who prosper
or fret about their wicked schemes.

PSALM 37:7 NLT

THE discipline of silence is hard for us because we go toe-to-toe and face-to-face with our need to control and fix things, while our Scripture in Psalms teaches us to do the exact opposite: "Be still in the presence of the Lord, and wait patiently for Him to act." This truth requires some silence on our part.

Some therapists call it the *seven-second count*, when you actually count in your mind to seven...meaning you don't open your mouth for seven seconds in order to let your client speak. The basic desire and need of all human beings is to be heard and understood, but if you do not leave space for both listening and speaking, that does not occur. God desires for us to go to Him and share our story because He truly cares and admonishes us to *be still and silently wait for Him to speak*. We will never be able to hear what God is saying if we continue talking and don't just sit in His presence. There is a time to be silent and a time to speak. God moments happen when we learn the art of both.

Tangible Takeaway ....

Sit in the presence of the Lord today...be still and patiently wait for Him to act. Be silent and listen to His still, small voice. Psalm 46:10 (NLT) says, "Be still, and know that I am God! I will be honored by every nation. I will be honored throughout the world." Write this verse on an index card as a reminder and place it in your Bible.

Choose kindness and laugh often.

—SUSAN GOSS

Short Memory

When he falls, he will not be hurled down,
because the LORD is the One who holds
his hand and sustains him.

PSALM 37:24 AMP

GREAT athletes learn over time to have short memories. They have to. They don't have time to dwell on a mistake—they must learn something from it, release it, and move on. Mia Hamm is a well-known United States soccer player who claims that, "Failure happens all the time. It happens every day in practice. What makes you better is how you react to it." Picture the gymnast on the balance beam performing at the Olympics. Imagine all the times she has flawlessly completed her routine, then in the performance of her lifetime she falls off the beam. She doesn't have time to hash out questions, "What just happened? What did I do wrong?" No—she absolutely must release it and move on immediately in order to finish her routine.

Her response to a mistake is everything. And so is ours. Many times in life when we have not responded well to mistakes we have made or haven't released hurtful memories or past pain to God, but instead tried to carry that burden around ourselves, the opposite takes place. And unlike the athlete that learns to release so they can become better, we remain the same. God desires for His people to live a life of abundance. "I came that they may have and enjoy life, and have it in abundance [to the full, till it overflows]" (John 10:10 AMP). If you desire to have a long memory, and memories can be wonderful, God so longs to be a part of your story. Maybe it's time to start releasing some of the past you've been carrying around today.

Tangible Takeaway

Is your memory short?

If not, what are you not releasing to God? Spend time with Jesus and ask Him with an open heart today.

True Friendship

A true friend loves regardless
of the situation, and a real brother
exists to share the tough times.

PROVERBS 17:17 THE VOICE

WOW, today's verse just stated that *a true friend loves regardless of the situation, and a real brother exists to share the tough times*...now that's some hardcore love because there can be an infinite number of situations that are both unpredictable or even disastrous that we can find ourselves in at just about any given time. C. S. Lewis once stated, "Friendship is the greatest of worldly goods. Certainly to me it is the chief happiness of life. If I had to give a piece of advice to a young man about a place to live, I think I should say, 'Sacrifice almost everything to live where you can be near your friends.'" Friend and brother are both valued. Proverbs 18:24 (The Voice) says, "But a true friend is closer than a brother." Friends that last a lifetime stick like *glue* during the good times and the bad because to them the *glue* that holds the friendship together is the connection of the heart *regardless of the situation*. Have you allowed God access to your heart as you reach out to connect with a friend?

Tangible Takeaway ··

Evaluate what kind of friend you are.

Are you faithful in times of adversity as well as prosperity?

Are you a "fair-weather" friend? There when all is well, but leaving when times get bad then flying back in during the good?

Might you need to write a letter to a friend?

Pray about these questions regarding your friends/ friendships and ask God if there is some action He wants you to take.

Busyness

Whatever you do,
do your work heartily,
as for the Lord
rather than for men.

COLOSSIANS 3:23 NASB

DID you know that there is a very good likelihood that you talk to the people at work more than you talk to the people you live with? Slow down and take a look at your spouse. Slow down and take a look at your child. Slow down and take a look at your friendships. *Just. Slow. Down.* Be intentional. "Whatever you do, do your work heartily, as for the Lord rather than for men" (Colossians 3:23 NASB). Sometimes we take that verse and do the very opposite because we are human and allow busyness and striving to take over. *We start to please men rather than God.* And when this happens, it is easy to get caught up in busyness and stop being intentional with those we are around. Busyness deceives us into believing we are accomplishing what the world says is necessary. It takes a daily Jesus download in order to keep us on track with His plan for us and those He has entrusted in our care. Proverbs 16:3 (AMP) tells us to "commit your works to the LORD [submit and trust them to Him], and your plans will succeed [if you respond to His will and guidance]."

Tangible Takeaway

The words "pleasing God over pleasing men" roll off the tongue so easily but are very difficult to live out. Take a fresh look at Colossians 3:23 as it relates to busyness, and ask yourself who you are trying to please...God or man?

Grieving Together

As they walked, Jesus wept; and everyone noticed
how much Jesus must have loved Lazarus.

JOHN 11:35–36 THE VOICE

ALTHOUGH Jesus grieved by weeping, grief has no formula. God knows loss, suffering, pain, and grief more than we could ever know. It is something that we cannot escape and that we will all experience at different times in our lives. Grief is sometimes referred to as an enigma because everyone grieves in their own unique way. Grief is not just about loss of life, but also about the loss of a job, a relationship, your health, an unmet expectation, and more. It is part of every relationship. But how do we grieve together in a healthy way?

The healthiest way to grieve is to grieve together in a relationship (marriage, friendships, etc.) and not isolate yourself. It is so important to share in the suffering together, yet not to judge or compare the stage of grief the other person is going through if it is not the same stage as yours. Everyone grieves differently—be patient, listen well, and pray, asking God to give you a discerning spirit. Processing and being curious with each other connects. For example, being intentional in checking in with each other...*How are you feeling? What are you working through right now?* And to sometimes just sit and not say anything...but to just let your presence be known.

Grieving not only draws us closer in relationship with others, but also ultimately to God. In times of grieving, it is critically important to go to the Savior and draw closer to Him...not pull away. "The LORD is close to the brokenhearted; He rescues those whose spirits are crushed" (Psalm 34:18 NLT). The Lord moves in close to revive us when we are grieving because He seeks to be our *comfort*. "God blesses those who mourn, for they will be comforted" (Matthew 5:4 NLT). God is the "merciful Father and the source of all comfort" (II Corinthians 1:3 NLT). He stands ready to wipe our tears (*Revelation 21:4*).

Tangible Takeaway

As everyone noticed how much Jesus loved Lazarus, so too God wants to share in our suffering and longs to be a part of our pain in order to restore us back to wholeness. Do you invite God into your suffering, or do you isolate and grieve alone?

Isomorphic: Same but Different

So let's keep focused on that goal, those of us who want
everything God has for us. If any of you have something
else in mind, something less than total commitment,
God will clear your blurred vision—you'll see it yet!
Now that we're on the right track, let's stay on it.

PHILIPPIANS 3:15—16 THE MESSAGE

THE word *isomorphic* can look intimidating, but it has a
simple meaning—yet it is not simple to implement. Why?
Because we are human. *Isomorphic* basically means
same but different. Our relationship with God should be
reflected in our relationships with each other...*same but
different.* If we stay focused on God, He will help us focus
in our relationships so that we do not get *blurred vision* but
stay *on the right track.* Other translations refer to "blurred
vision" as "distractions"—which we are most familiar with.
We can all relate with Peter in Matthew 14:25–31 (NASB):

> And in the fourth watch of the night He came to
> them, walking on the sea. When the disciples saw Him

walking on the sea, they were terrified, and said, "It is a ghost!" And they cried out in fear. But immediately Jesus spoke to them, saying, "Take courage, it is I; do not be afraid." Peter said to Him, "Lord, if it is You, command me to come to You on the water." And He said, "Come!" And Peter got out of the boat, and walked on the water and came toward Jesus. But seeing the wind, he became frightened, and beginning to sink, he cried out, "Lord, save me!" Immediately Jesus stretched out His hand and took hold of him, and said to him, "You of little faith, why did you doubt?"

Peter believed that he could walk on water because he believed in Jesus and Jesus told him to come. But when Peter took his eyes off of Jesus, He immediately began to sink. Isn't it interesting that when our focus is on the problem, the problem just gets bigger. But when our focus is on God, God gets bigger.

Tangible Takeaway

Peter's faith was isomorphic because his faith was strong enough to get out of the boat, but like us, he was human and got distracted. Is your focus on your problem? Or is your focus on God? Ask God to help you keep focused on the goal so that you can remain totally committed.

Forgiveness

But if we own up to our sins, God shows that He is faithful and just by forgiving us of our sins and purifying us from the pollution of all the bad things we have done.

I JOHN 1:9 THE VOICE

FORGIVENESS researcher Robert Enright says, "Forgiving begins with acknowledging that we are people who have a right to be treated with respect. Forgiving does not require denying that we have been hurt. On the contrary, to forgive we have to admit that we have been hurt and that we have a right to feel hurt, angry, or resentful. Forgiving does not require denying our feelings."[15] This is such a powerful quote because it gives us purpose and reason to feel our feelings and emotions that are attached to our pain. In doing this, we are able to identify what it is that we need to forgive.

Forgiveness is a process that we begin with God because it brings freedom. Unforgiveness keeps us in bondage. The enemy hates it when we forgive because it ushers him out and creates healthy relationships that reflect Jesus. God's forgiveness is "as far as the east is from the west" (Psalm 103:12 NASB). God forgives and forgets. Man's forgiveness does not work that way because we *do* have a memory.

Therefore, we must go to God daily and sometimes moment by moment to release our *hurt, anger, and resentfulness* so we can *graciously forgive.* Until we are free from the pain and poison of unforgiveness, we need to continue the releasing process, day by day, until God frees us.

Tangible Takeaway ·······································

Read these Scriptures:

"Instead, be kind and compassionate. Graciously forgive one another just as God has forgiven you through the Anointed, our Liberating King." —Ephesians 4:32 The Voice

Are you kind and compassionate? Do you graciously forgive?

"When you pray, if you remember anyone who has wronged you, forgive him so that God above can also forgive you." —Mark 11:25 The Voice

Are you reminded of anyone who has wronged you when you pray? Have you prayed for them?

"Put up with one another. Forgive. Pardon any offenses against one another, as the Lord has pardoned you, because you should act in kind." —Colossians 3:13 The Voice

Have you offended anyone, or has anyone offended you that you need to pardon and forgive?

Love Your Neighbor as Yourself

The second great commandment is this:
"Love others in the same way you love yourself."

MARK 12:31 THE VOICE

WHO'S your neighbor? God says *everyone* is. "The central truth—the one you have heard since the beginning of your faith—is that we must love one another" (I John 3:11 The Voice). But did you catch in today's Scripture, we are not only to *love others*...but *love others in the same way we love ourselves*. First, we must know and believe that God loves us so that we can then love others. "We love because He has first loved us" (I John 4:19 The Voice). Next, through knowing and believing God's love for us, we are able to then *love each other deeply and fully* as Jesus has loved us. "So I give you a new command: Love each other deeply and fully. Remember the ways that I have loved you, and demonstrate your love for others in those same ways" (John 13:34 The Voice). Finally, just think about how you would love your neighbor better if you had a healthy love for yourself.

Yes, we are called to love others, but you cannot stop there—we are to love others in the *same way* we love ourselves. Loving our neighbor will not always be easy because our neighbors are imperfect people, as are we. God is the connector that loves through us. *We love because He has first loved us.*

Tangible Takeaway

"We love because He has first loved us" (I John 4:19 The Voice).

This powerful yet simple truth is paramount to living out our faith.

"So I give you a new command: Love each other deeply and fully. Remember the ways that I have loved you, and demonstrate your love for others in those same ways" (John 13:34 The Voice).

Do you demonstrate your love for others without judgment and meet people where they are like Jesus did?

"The second great commandment is this: 'Love others in the same way you love yourself' " (Mark 12:31 The Voice).

How do you know you love yourself?

The Big Three

He has told you, O man, what is good;
And what does the LORD require of you
But to do justice, to love kindness,
And to walk humbly with your God?

MICAH 6:8 NASB

DO you have a biblical worldview that guides you in decision-making, how you treat others, and becomes the filter in which you see the world? Micah 6:8 is an excellent start if you're looking. In every relationship and decision that we make, we ultimately want God to be pleased, even happy, right? So how does that happen? God is pleased, and yes, even happy, when we *do justice, love kindness, and walk humbly with* Him. This is the complete opposite of pride, which is where our human nature tends to lead us. We cannot be prideful and humble with a sincere heart at the same time. Our divided heart cannot take it, which eventually causes us to become spiritually sick. By inviting God into helping us live out *doing justice, loving kindness, and walking humbly with* Him, a life full of compassion for others is the natural overflow of this biblical worldview. Is it hard? Yes, but all beautiful things generally take time to grow. Galatians 6:9–10 (ESV) says, "And let us not grow weary of doing good, for in due season we will reap, if we do not give up. So then, as we have opportunity, let us do good to everyone, and especially to those who are of the household of faith."

Tangible Takeaway

In your mirror moment with God today, divide up Micah 6:8 into sections.

"He has told you, O man, what is good; and what does the Lord require of you…"

"But to do justice": Ask God, "What am I doing for justice?"

"To love kindness": Ask God, "Do I 'love' kindness?" It is easy to love kindness when people are kind to you… but what about when they are harsh? Do you still "love" kindness?

"To walk humbly with your God": Ask God, "Am I inviting You into every hour, minute, and second of each day and life moment?"

We're Still in This

Jesus Christ is the same
yesterday, today, and forever.

HEBREWS 13:8 NLT

SOMETIMES we just need to hear the words "we're still in this" to make us feel secure. To say it expresses security and to receive it brings a more confident layer of hope and stability to any relationship. It's so reassuring to know during those moments in life that are really messy and hard (*you know, the ones that never get posted on Instagram when life is real and raw and definitely not photo worthy*) that someone would stop and affirm their commitment to the relationship and each other with four small words, "We're still in this." Our Scripture today makes us feel secure in a Savior that will always be near. In our humanness we become fickle, and the meaning of commitment can begin to fade, but Jesus is the same always. A. Solid. Rock. "I love You, LORD; You are my strength. The LORD is my rock, my fortress, and my Savior; my God is my rock, in whom I find protection.

He is my shield, the power that saves me, and my place of safety" (Psalm 18:1–2 NLT). When we are fickle, God never is. When we feel insecure, God is a Rock of security. When we need a reminder of hope and stability in our relationships, we can begin with four small words, *"We're still in this."*

Tangible Takeaway

••

Are you in a messy spot and need some reassurance in your relationship? Do you need a reminder of hope and stability? Try introducing these four words into your relationship, "We're still in this." Thank God that He is not fickle but instead is our hope, our security, and our stability because Jesus Christ is the same yesterday, today, and forever.

Cheerfully Expectant

Don't burn out; keep yourselves fueled and aflame.
Be alert servants of the Master, cheerfully expectant.
Don't quit in hard times; pray all the harder. Help needy
Christians; be inventive in hospitality. Bless your enemies;
no cursing under your breath. Laugh with your happy
friends when they're happy; share tears when they're
down. Get along with each other; don't be stuck-up.
Make friends with nobodies; don't be the great somebody.
Don't hit back; discover beauty in everyone.
If you've got it in you, get along with everybody.
Don't insist on getting even; that's not for you to do.
"I'll do the judging," says God. "I'll take care of it."

ROMANS 12:11—21 THE MESSAGE

OUR Scripture tell us that if you see your enemy hungry, go buy that person lunch, or if he's thirsty, get him a drink. Your generosity will surprise him with goodness. Don't let evil get the best of you; get the best of evil by doing good.

Wow, to be *cheerfully expectant* that God can do what we cannot within our own strength each day is in fact a GREAT way to start each day, don't you think? God wants it all...not just in part. Being *cheerfully expectant* means to have an expectant faith that knows God desires to do more than we would ever ask. The *cheerfully expectant* life is an intentional life of leaning into Jesus daily for the answers we need both relationally and practically...with an expectant faith that He will work. God wants to show up, show off, and sell out in our lives. And if we're expecting Him to show up, there is no limit to what God can do!

Tangible Takeaway

Read out loud Romans 12:11–21. Let it serve as an expectant reminder that it is not us...it is Him!

*My response
to another human being
is not based on their behavior
but on where I am
in my relationship
with Jesus.*

—SUSAN GOSS

Flesh

I don't really understand myself, for I want to do what is right, but I don't do it. Instead, I do what I hate. But if I know that what I am doing is wrong, this shows that I agree that the law is good. So I am not the one doing wrong; it is sin living in me that does it. And I know that nothing good lives in me, that is, in my sinful nature. I want to do what is right, but I can't. I want to do what is good, but I don't. I don't want to do what is wrong, but I do it anyway. But if I do what I don't want to do, I am not really the one doing wrong; it is sin living in me that does it.

ROMANS 7:15—20 NLT

IN every relationship at some point we all find ourselves saying, "I can't believe I did that...I can't believe I said that...I knew I shouldn't have, but I did anyway." Human nature seems to always find a way to sneak out and raise its ugly head, even when we want to be doing good. It is a natural yet constant battle in the mind saying to oneself, *I want to do what is right, but I can't.* The Voice translation even calls out our human nature, "But now

I am no longer the one acting—I've lost control—sin has taken up residence in me and is wreaking havoc" (Romans 7:17). Even though the fight is against human nature, it is a battle worth fighting and one we must constantly be linked to God with in order to win. So... how do you fight your battles?

Tangible Takeaway

Just like our Scripture verse repeats the conflict of our human nature, when you find yourself fighting the battle within, think about your focus. Remember, the more we focus on our struggle/problem, the bigger it becomes in our minds and can sometimes overtake us. The more we focus on GOD, the bigger HE becomes in our hearts and minds and overtakes us! Pray and ask God to help you with your focus.

Projection

*Timothy, do everything you can to present yourself
to God as a man who is fully genuine, a worker unashamed
of your mission, a guide capable of leading others along
the correct path defined by the word of truth.*

II TIMOTHY 2:15 THE VOICE

IN therapy the word *projection* is "a psychological defense mechanism in which individuals attribute characteristics they find unacceptable in themselves to another person. For example, a husband who has a hostile nature might attribute this hostility to his wife and say she has an anger management problem."[16] Psychological projection is "a defense mechanism people subconsciously employ in order to cope with difficult feelings or emotions. Psychological projection involves projecting undesirable feelings or emotions onto someone else, rather than admitting to or dealing with the unwanted feelings."[17]

As you can see, our relationships are as healthy as we are individually. It's true. If we are unhealthy emotionally and spiritually, it's pretty fair to say we tend to want to blame *someone else* for just about any failure we see in our own life. This happens because we are frustrated with ourselves, which then just makes us frustrated with everyone. The opposite, however, is equally true. If we stay close to God each day and reflect His image, then we can be more *fully genuine, a worker unashamed, leading others along the correct path defined by the word of truth.*

Tangible Takeaway

Reread the definition of projection above. Ask God if you have been projecting onto others what you need God to change in and through you.

United Front

Here is one thing that would complete my joy—come together as one in mind and spirit and purpose, sharing in the same love.

PHILIPPIANS 2:2 THE VOICE

DECISIONS can sometimes be hard. When two people are trying to make a decision together, it can be even harder. In marriage, it is critical that each validate the opinion of the other and that both feel heard and understood. When God is invited into the process first, it puts Him in the position where He should be and "us" in a posture that allows us to follow as we ask Him to lead. When I feel "heard and understood" about why I do or don't want something, and then I listen to you to hear why you do or don't want something, and we don't move forward until we are unified on that issue...that connects us. It does not necessarily mean we are getting what we might think we want, but we do agree that it is best for our connection and we are unified on that. Then and only then do we move forward with that particular decision.

A connection that comes from achieving a united front flows out of a shared love for each other, but first a shared love of seeking God. "But above all these, put on love! Love is the perfect tie to bind these together" (Colossians 3:14 The Voice).

Tangible Takeaway

It is so important for us to ask God to help us come together as one in mind and spirit and purpose, sharing in the same love. Take a look at the questions below and, as you answer them, allow God to reveal to you where your heart condition is as you answer.

Using Merriam-Webster's definition of united front, do you join together and have a shared goal with a group of people or organization?

Do you seek God first to guide you in the decision-making process?

Do you value the opinions of others...even when they are different from yours?

Embracing Imperfection

Not a single person on earth
is always good and never sins.

ECCLESIASTES 7:20 NLT

I love you just the way you are. Jesus loved people that way. He didn't try to change them, guilt trip them, or shame them. He just loved them...plain and simple. To embrace each other's imperfections is a great model to live by, isn't it? Accepting the fact that we are not perfect helps us understand that others are not perfect either. This allows us to accept their imperfections and hope they will embrace ours as well. Not trying to change the ones we do life with is the key to opening our hearts for God to work in us. Allowing Him to do so creates a space to fully embrace them as they are. For Scripture lets us know that "we all make many mistakes. For if we could control our tongues, we would be perfect

and could also control ourselves in every other way"
(James 3:2 NLT).

Tangible Takeaway

Sit alone with God and ask the following questions:

- *Do you find yourself being manipulative in relationships instead of embracing them at face value?*

- *Are you trying to change others into who you want them to be rather than who God made them to be?*

Learning to embrace the imperfections of ourselves and the people we do life with helps us to understand that "we all make many mistakes" (James 3:2 NLT) and "not a single person on earth is always good and never sins" (Ecclesiastes 7:20 NLT). Ask God to help you accept others with open arms.

Take One, Take Two

Then Peter came to Him and asked,
"Lord, how often should I forgive someone
who sins against me? Seven times?"
"NO, not seven times," Jesus replied,
"but seventy times seven!"

MATTHEW 18:21—22 NLT

ALTHOUGH a play on words, our verse today is a reminder of how the world most commonly views forgiveness. As an illustration, take, for instance, what the movie industry refers to as *take one*...it goes something like this: "In the movie business, 'take one' is the first try at filming a particular scene. It is what is called out at the beginning. If the actors mess up the lines, etc., it will go to 'take two' or 'take three' or 'take forty-seven'" (Urban Dictionary). Have you ever been hurt by someone in a relationship? Betrayed? Sabotaged? Rejected? If you ever have, you know the pain that it causes. The knot it can keep your soul tied up in. And that the only way to *untie* the knot is to forgive the offender—because forgiveness begins not only the healing but also the freeing process. And because forgiveness is a process, just like the movie industry refers to *take one* as the beginning of the process, if we mess up and still harbor unforgiveness, it might require a *take two* or *take three* or even a *take forty-seven* sometimes before our hearts are softened and changed from hearts of unforgiveness and bitterness to hearts of forgiveness and freedom. Bondage or freedom—you choose!

Tangible Takeaway

Have you ever thought that forgiveness is a one-time event?

Or perhaps the opposite is true. How many takes have you had in a particular relationship?

Ask God to reveal Himself to you and show you His truth about forgiveness—one relationship at a time.

Bonds in Friendships

Don't let selfishness and prideful agendas take over.
Embrace true humility, and lift your heads
to extend love to others. Get beyond yourselves
and protecting your own interests; be sincere,
and secure your neighbors' interests first.
PHILIPPIANS 2:3—4 THE VOICE

WHAT is the real *bond* of your friendships? In other words, what's the glue that holds the friendship together? It's a good question to ask because bonds can be healthy or unhealthy. A bond can be made because of a shared love of Jesus, family, a common interest or hobby, or even work. These are all examples of healthy bonding. However, a bond can also be made because of shared addictions in gambling, alcohol, or sex—all examples of unhealthy bonding. Our word reminds us beautifully today through Scripture to not let *selfishness* and *prideful* agendas take over and to look outside of ourselves. Do you regard one another as more important than yourselves, or are you looking out for number one?

We are reminded to build each other up. A healthy bond does not need something outside of the relationship as an object of its attention for the bond to work. The bond IS each other with God as the glue holding it together.

Tangible Takeaway

Given the examples above for healthy and unhealthy bonds in friendships, assess your own. Do you bond for healthy or unhealthy reasons? Ask yourself these questions:

- *Am I selfish or prideful?*
- *Do I embrace true humility?*
- *Do I extend love to others?*
- *Am I sincere?*
- *Do I secure my neighbors' interests first?*

What Are You Looking at?

*But first and most importantly seek
(aim at, strive after) His kingdom and
His righteousness [His way of doing
and being right—the attitude
and character of God], and all these
things will be given to you also.*

MATTHEW 6:33 AMP

WHETHER it's the newest products that meet our every want or need or a new food discovered that could satisfy our indulgent taste buds, we are surrounded day in and day out with flashy things that are all vying for our attention. It's so easy to get distracted these days. If we are not intentional about our focus on God, we could get lost very quickly on the minutiae of details in front of us and allow that to be our focus. But God says, "Seek Me first....and all these things will be given to you also."

So what are you looking at? Like aiming at a bull's-eye with laser focus, if we keep our eyes on Him, it keeps our souls away from chaos. Bottom line—it is ALL about Jesus. Just look at Him!

Tangible Takeaway

Personalize this Scripture:

But first _____(your name)_____ and most importantly _(your name)_ seek His kingdom _(your name)_ and His righteousness _(your name)_ and all these things _(your name)_ will be given to you also _(your name)_.

Take note of the definition of "seek" in the Scripture above. Ask yourself, "Do I aim at or strive after God, His kingdom, and His righteousness?"

Take note of the definition of "righteousness" in the Scripture above. Ask yourself, "Am I representing Christ well? Do I have the attitude and character of God in my life?"

The Heart's Motive

Every man's way is right in his own eyes,
but the Lord weighs and examines the hearts
[of people and their motives].

PROVERBS 21:2 AMP

WHY do we do what we do, and who are we doing it for? Is it for man or for God? If the answer is man, then we have lived on the hamster wheel that turns continuously and we know the feeling one has when they cannot get off. This is because with man we are always wanting to please, but we soon find out it is never enough. Yet we continue to try... thus the hamster wheel of life spinning out of control. Even good stuff can spin out of control, like volunteering at a local food shelter, leading a small group at church, or being active in a local philanthropic organization. It is all a matter of the heart. Take a look at Matthew 6:1 (AMP), "Be [very] careful not to do your good deeds publicly, to be seen by men; otherwise you will have no reward [prepared and awaiting you] with your Father who is in heaven." It is a great reminder because sometimes we get caught up in doing what is good so that we can feel better about ourselves or for the benefit of others to see. Yet God looks at the heart. "But the LORD weighs and examines the hearts [of people and their motives]" (Proverbs 21:2 AMP). So the question remains: Are we trying to please ourselves, others, or God?

Tangible Takeaway

One important question today as you go before the Lord:

Why do you do what you do, and who are you doing it for?

Valuing All People

Show respect for all people
[treat them honorably],
love the brotherhood [of believers],
fear God, honor the king.

I PETER 2:17 AMP

DO you know how to place value on another human being? How to show respect for ALL people by treating them honorably? The Bible says, "Be kind to one another, tenderhearted, forgiving one another, as God in Christ forgave you" (Ephesians 4:32 ESV). It also states "And as you wish that others would do to you, do so to them" (Luke 6:31 ESV). In neither reference, you find "only be tenderhearted to those who agree with you" or "only treat the people you like as you would like to be treated." They don't say that. In fact, Jesus' life teaches us to show value and respect for ALL people. So many times we lose sight of what the word *value* means as it relates to *people* and think of it only in relation to *monetary worth*. The definition of value is "the regard that something" is held to deserve; the importance, worth, or usefulness of something.

"This is what our Scriptures come to teach: in everything, in every circumstance, do to others as you would have them do to you" (Matthew 7:12 The Voice). God values ALL people, and that includes us. Are we living like God values us by valuing the relationships we are in?

Tangible Takeaway

How we value ALL human beings reveals our relationship with God. It is isomorphic—same but different. Read Psalm 139 in its entirety to see the value God places on you. Live like you are valued by God so you can "show respect for all people [treat them honorably]."

Potential Energy

So God created human beings
in His own image.
In the image of God He created them;
male and female He created them.

GENESIS 1:27 NLT

WE are all created in the image of God. Therefore, we all have a potential created inside of us. There is a scientific term called *potential energy* which means "the stored energy an object has because of its position or state."[18] For example, a battery by itself does not do anything, but when in use, it releases its stored energy...its full potential. Electricity to your home has potential. When you flip a switch or plug something into an outlet, you see its energy released. So if *we are created in the image of God,* then we are born with potential, and just like a battery and electricity we, too, have to be positioned or plugged in to tap it. Then it is a natural progression to reach out and help others reach their potential too. "So encourage each other and build each other up, just as you are already doing" (I Thessalonians 5:11 NLT).

Tangible Takeaway ··

Have you ever thought of yourself as potential energy?
What are you plugged into? Is it healthy or unhealthy?
Are you helping bring out the potential in others?
In your relationships, do you point each other to God or each other?

Read Genesis 1:27 out loud with your name inserted as a prayer:

So God created   (your name)   in His own image. In the image of God He created   (your name) ; male and female He created them.

*Why do you look at the speck
that is in your brother's eye,
but do not notice the log that is
in your own eye? Or how can you
say to your brother, "Let me take
the speck out of your eye,"
and behold, the log is in your own
eye? You hypocrite, first take the log
out of your own eye, and then
you will see clearly to take the speck
out of your brother's eye.*

MATTHEW 7:3–5 NASB

Notes

1. Lysa TerKeurst, *Uninvited: Living Loved When You Feel Less Than, Left Out, and Lonely* (Nashville: Thomas Nelson, 2016), 261.

2. Gerald Corey, *Theory and Practice of Counseling and Psychotherapy*, 7th ed. (Stamford: Thomson, 2005), 60.

3. Robert I. Sutton, "When NBA Players Touch Teammates More, They Win More," Psychology Today, December 21, 2010, https://www.psychologytoday.com/us/blog/work-matters/201012/when-nba-players-touch-teammates-more-they-win-more.

4. Louanne Ward, "The Power of Touch in Relationships," LinkedIn, April 12, 2016, https://www.linkedin.com/pulse/power-touch-relationships-louanne-ward.

5. Lawrence Robinson, Melinda Smith, and Jeanne Segal, "Laughter Is the Best Medicine: The Health Benefits of Humor and Laughter," HelpGuide, updated November 2018, https://www.helpguide.org/articles/mental-health/laughter-is-the-best-medicine.htm.

6. Ecclesia Bible Society. *The Voice Bible* (Nashville: Thomas Nelson, 2013), 1152.

7. Gary Chapman, "Receiving Gifts," The 5 Love Languages, accessed April 4, 2019, https://www.5lovelanguages.com/languages/receiving-gifts/.

8. Nicholas Sparks, *The Notebook*, directed by Nick Cassavetes (Burbank, CA: New Line Cinema, 2004), DVD.

9. Ian Morgan Cron, Suzanne Stabile, *The Road Back to You: An Enneagram Journey to Self-Discovery* (Westmont: InterVarsity Press, 2016), book jacket copy.

10. Mayo Clinic Staff, "Stress Relief from Laughter? It's No Joke," Mayo Clinic, April 21, 2016, https://www.mayoclinic.org/healthy-lifestyle/stress-management/in-depth/stress-relief/art-20044456.

11. Kyle Benson, "The Magic Relationship Ratio, According to Science," *The Gottman Institute* (blog), October 4, 2017, https://www.gottman.com/blog/the-magic-relationship-ratio-according-science/.

12. "A Lesson in Customer Service from Chick-fil-A President Dan Cathy," SAS, SAS Institute, Inc., accessed February 26, 2019, https://www.sas.com/en_us/insights/articles/marketing/a-lesson-in-customer-service-from-chick-fil-a.html.

13. Erwin McManus, *Uprising: A Revolution of the Soul* (Nashville: Thomas Nelson, 2003), 251.

14. Carole Bos, "Derek Redmond: The Day that Changed My Life," Awesome Stories, updated June 19, 2017, https://www.awesomestories.com/asset/view/Derek-Redmond-The-Day-that-Changed-My-Life.

15. Robert Enright, *Forgiveness is a Choice: A Step-by-Step Process for Resolving Anger and Restoring Hope* (Washington DC: American Psychological Association, 2001), 23, 24

16. "Projection," *GoodTherapy* (blog), updated February 16, 2016, https://www.goodtherapy.org/blog/psychpedia/projection.

17. "Psychological Projection: Dealing with Undesirable Emotions," Everyday Health, updated November 15, 2017, https://www.everydayhealth.com/emotional-health/psychological-projection-dealing-with-undesirable-emotions/.

18. Ken Nelson, "Physics for Kids: Potential Energy," Ducksters, Technological Solutions, Inc., accessed February 26, 2019, https://www.ducksters.com/science/physics/potential_energy.php.

LIVE YOUR FAITH

Dear Friend,

This book was prayerfully crafted with you, the reader, in mind—every word, every sentence, every page— was thoughtfully written, designed, and packaged to encourage you...right where you are this very moment. At DaySpring, our vision is to see every person experience the life-changing message of God's love. So, as we worked through rough drafts, design changes, edits, and details, we prayed for you to deeply experience His unfailing love, indescribable peace, and pure joy. It is our sincere hope that through these Truth-filled pages your heart will be blessed, knowing that God cares about you—your desires and disappointments, your challenges and dreams.

He knows. He cares. He loves you unconditionally.

BLESSINGS!
THE DAYSPRING BOOK TEAM

**Additional copies of this book and
other DaySpring titles can be purchased
at fine bookstores everywhere.
Order online at <u>dayspring.com</u>
or
by phone at 1-877-751-4347**